HUGH

But there is more than I can see,
And what I see I leave unsaid,
Nor speak it, knowing Death has made
His darkness beautiful with thee.

ROBERT HUGH BENSON

IN 1912. AGED 40

In the robes of a Papal Chamberlain.

HUGH

MEMOIRS OF A BROTHER

BY

ARTHUR CHRISTOPHER BENSON

NEW IMPRESSION

LONGMANS, GREEN, AND CO.

FOURTH AVENUE & 30TH STREET, NEW YORK

1915

PREFACE

THIS book was begun with no hope or intention of making a formal and finished biography, but only to place on record some of my brother's sayings and doings, to fix scenes and memories before they suffered from any dim obliteration of time, to catch, if I could, for my own comfort and delight, the tone and sense of that vivid and animated atmosphere which Hugh always created about him. His arrival upon any scene was never in the smallest degree uproarious, and still less was it in the least mild or serene; yet he came into a settled circle like a freshet of tumbling water into a still pool!

I knew all along that I could not attempt any account of what may be called his public life, which all happened since he became a Roman Catholic. He passed through many circles — in England, in Rome, in America — of which I knew nothing. I never heard him make a public speech, and I only once heard him preach since he ceased to be an Anglican. This was not because I thought he would convert me, nor because I shrank from hearing him preach a doctrine to which I did not adhere, nor for any sectarian reason. Indeed, I regret not having heard him preach and speak oftener; it would have interested me, and it would have been kinder and more brotherly; but one is apt not to do the things which one thinks one can always do, and the fact that I did not hear him was due to a mixture of shyness and laziness, which I now regret in vain.

But I think that his life as a Roman Catholic ought to be written fully and carefully, because there were many people who trusted and admired and loved him as a priest who would wish to have some record of his days. He left me, by a will, which we are carrying out, though it was not duly executed, all his letters, papers,

and manuscripts, and we have arranged
to have an official biography of him written, and have placed all his papers in the
hands of a Catholic biographer, Father
C. C. Martindale, S.J.

Since Hugh died I have read a good
many notices of him, which have appeared
mostly in Roman Catholic organs. These
were, as a rule, written by people who had
only known him as a Catholic, and gave
an obviously incomplete view of his character and temperament. It could not well
have been otherwise, but the result was
that only one side of a very varied and
full life was presented. He was depicted
in a particular office and in a specific mood.
This was certainly his most real and eager
mood, and deserves to be emphasized.
But he had other moods and other sides,
and his life before he became a Catholic
had a charm and vigour of its own.

Moreover, his family affection was very
strong; when he became a Catholic, we all
of us felt, including himself, that there
might be a certain separation, not of

affection, but of occupations and interests;
and he himself took very great care to
avoid this, with the happy result that we
saw him, I truly believe, more often and
more intimately than ever before. Indeed,
my own close companionship with him
really began when he came first as a
Roman Catholic to Cambridge.

And so I have thought it well to draw in
broad strokes and simple outlines a picture of his personality as we, his family,
knew and loved it. It is only a *study*, so
to speak, and is written very informally
and directly. Formal biographies, as I
know from experience, must emphasise a
different aspect. They deal, as they are
bound to do, with public work and official
activities; and the personal atmosphere
often vanishes in the process — that subtle
essence of quality, the effect of a man's
talk and habits and prejudices and pre-
dispositions, which comes out freely in
private life, and is even suspended in his
public ministrations. It would be impossible, I believe, to make a presentment of

PREFACE

Hugh which could be either dull or conventional. But, on the other hand, his life as a priest, a writer, a teacher, a controversialist, was to a certain extent governed and conditioned by circumstances; and I can see, from many accounts of him, that the more intimate and unrestrained side of him can only be partially discerned by those who knew him merely in an official capacity.

That, then, is the history of this brief Memoir. It is just an attempt to show Hugh as he showed himself, freely and unaffectedly, to his own circle; and I am sure that this deserves to be told, for the one characteristic which emerges whenever I think of him is that of a beautiful charm, not without a touch of wilfulness and even petulance about it, which gave him a childlike freshness, a sparkling zest, that aerated and enlivened all that he did or said. It was a charm which made itself instantly felt, and yet it could be hardly imitated or adopted, because it was so entirely unconscious and unaffected. He enjoyed enacting his part, and he was as instinctively and whole-heartedly a priest as another man is a soldier or a lawyer. But his function did not wholly occupy and dominate his life; and, true priest though he was, the force and energy of his priesthood came at least in part from the fact that he was entirely and delightfully human, and I deeply desire that this should not be overlooked or forgotten.

A. C. B.

TREMANS, HORSTED KEYNES,
December 26, 1914.

CONTENTS

I

HARE STREET

HUGH

[xii]

CONTENTS

HUGH

XIX
RETROSPECT

XX
ATTAINMENT

XXI
TEMPERAMENT

LIST OF ILLUSTRATIONS

"Then said *Great-heart* to **Mr.** *Valiant-for-Truth*, Thou hast worthily behaved thyself. Let me see thy Sword. So he shewed it him. When he had taken it in his hand, and looked thereon a while, he said, *Ha, it is a right Jerusalem Blade!*"

The Pilgrim's Progress.

HUGH

I
HARE STREET

HOW loudly and boisterously the wind roared to-day across the low-hung, cloud-smeared sky, driving the broken rack before it, warm and wet out of the south! What a wintry landscape! leafless trees bending beneath the onset of the wind, bare and streaming hedges, pale close-reaped wheat-fields, brown ploughland, spare pastures stretching away to left and right, softly rising and falling to the horizon; nothing visible but distant belts of trees and coverts, with here and there the tower of a hidden church overtopping them, and a windmill or two; on the left, long lines of willows marking the course of a stream. The road soaked with rain, the grasses heavy with it, hardly a human being to be seen.

HUGH

I came at last to a village straggling
along each side of the road; to the right,
a fantastic-looking white villa, with many
bow-windows, and an orchard behind it.
Then on the left, a great row of beeches
on the edge of a pasture; and then, over
the barns and ricks of a farm, 'rose the
clustered chimneys of an old house; and
soon we drew up at a big iron gate between
tall red-brick gateposts; beyond it a paling,
with a row of high lime trees bordering a
garden lawn, and on beyond that the irregular village street.

From the gate a little flagged pathway
leads up to the front of a long, low house,
of mellow brick, with a solid cornice and
parapet, over which the tiled roof is visible:
a door in the centre, with two windows on
each side and five windows above — just
the sort of house that you find in a cathedral close.   To the left of the iron gate are
two other tall gateposts, with a road leading up to the side of the house, and a yard
with a row of stables behind.

Let me describe the garden first.   All

HARE STREET HOUSE

FROM THE FRONT 1914

The room to the left of the door is the dining room, with Hugh's bedroom over it. To the right of the door is the library.

along the front and south side of the house
runs a flagged pathway, a low brick wall
dividing it from the lawn, with plants in
rough red pots on little pilasters at intervals. To the right, as we face the door,
the lawn runs along the road, and stretches
back into the garden. There are tall,
lopped lime-trees all round the lawn, in
the summer making a high screen of
foliage, but now bare. If we take the
flagged path round the house, turn the corner, and go towards the garden, the yew
trees grow thick and close, forming an
arched walk at the corner, half screen-
ing an old irregular building of woodwork
and plaster, weather-boarded in places,
with a tiled roof, connected with the house
by a little covered cloister with wooden
pillars. If we pass that by, pursuing the
path among the yew trees, we come out
on a pleasant orchard, with a few flower-
beds, thickly encircled by shrubs, beyond
which, towards the main road, lies a com-
fortable-looking old red-brick cottage, with
a big barn and a long garden, which evi-

dently belongs to the larger house, because a gate in the paling stands open. Then there is another little tiled building behind the shrubs, where you can hear an engine at work, for electric light and water-pumping, and beyond that again, but still connected with the main house, stands another house among trees, of rough-cast and tiles, with an open wooden gallery, in a garden of its own.

In the orchard itself is a large grass-grown mound, with a rough wooden cross on the top; and down below that, in the orchard, is a newly-made grave, still covered, as I saw it to-day, with wreaths of leaves and moss, tied some of them with stained purple ribbons. The edge of the grave-mound is turfed, but the bare and trodden grass shows that many feet have crossed and recrossed the ground.

The orchard is divided on the left from a further and larger garden by a dense growth of old hazels; and passing through an alley you see that a broad path runs concealed among the hazels, a pleasant

Photo by Bishop, Barkway

HARE STREET HOUSE

FROM THE GARDEN 1914

The timbered building on the left is the Chapel;
in the foreground is the unfinished rose-garden.

shady walk in summer heat. Then the
larger garden stretches in front of you;
it is a big place, with rows of vegetables,
fruit-trees, and flower-borders, screened to
the east by a row of elms and dense shrubberies of laurel. Along the north runs a
high red-brick wall, with a big old-fashioned vine-house in the centre, of careful
design. In the corner nearest the house
is a large rose-garden, with a brick pedestal
in the centre, behind which rises the back
of the stable, also of old red brick.

But now there is a surprise; the back
of the house is much older than the front.
You see that it is a venerable Tudor building, with pretty panels of plaster embossed
with a rough pattern. The moulded brick
chimney-stacks are Tudor too, while the
high gables cluster and lean together with
a picturesque outline. The back of the
house forms a little court, with the cloister
of which I spoke before running round
two sides of it. Another great yew tree
stands there: while a doorway going into
the timber and plaster building which I

mentioned before has a rough device on it of a papal tiara and keys, carved in low relief and silvered.

A friendly black collie comes out of a kennel and desires a little attention. He licks my hand and looks at me with melting brown eyes, but has an air of expecting to see someone else as well. A black cat comes out of a door, runs beside us, and when picked up, clasps my shoulder contentedly and purrs in my ear.

The house seen from the back looks exactly what it is, a little old family mansion of a line of small squires, who farmed their own land, and lived on their own produce, though the barns and rick-yard belong to the house no longer. The red-brick front is just an addition made for the sake of stateliness at some time of prosperity. It is a charming self-contained little place, with a forgotten family tradition of its own, a place which could twine itself about the heart, and be loved and remembered by children brought up there, when far away. There is no sign of wealth about it, but every sign of ease and comfort and simple dignity.

Now we will go back to the front door and go through the house itself. The door opens into a tiny hall lighted by the glass panes of the door, and bright with pictures — oil paintings and engravings. The furniture old and sturdy, and a few curiosities about — carvings, weapons, horns of beasts. To the left a door opens into a pleasant dining-room, with two windows looking out in front, dark as dining-rooms may well be. It is hung with panels of green cloth, it has a big open Tudor fireplace, with a big oak settle, some china on an old dresser, a solid table and chairs, and a hatch in the corner through which dishes can be handed.

Opposite, on the other side of the hall, a door opens into a long low library, with books all round in white shelves. There is a big grand piano here, a very solid narrow oak table with a chest below, a bureau, and some comfortable chintz-covered chairs with a deep sofa. A per-

fect room to read or to hear music in,
with its two windows to the front, and a
long window opening down to the ground
at the south end. All the books here are
catalogued, and each has its place. If you
go out into the hall again and pass through,
a staircase goes up into the house, the walls
of it panelled, and hung with engravings;
some of the panels are carved with holy
emblems. At the foot of the stairs a door
on the right takes you into a small sitting-
room, with a huge stone fireplace; a big
window looks south, past the dark yew
trees, on to the lawn. There are little
devices in the quarries of the window, and
a deep window-seat. The room is hung
with a curious tapestry, brightly coloured
mediæval figures standing out from a dark
background. There is not room for much
furniture here; a square oak stand for
books, a chair or two by the fire. Par-
allel to the wall, with a chair behind it
filling up much of the space, is a long,
solid old oak table, set out for writing. It
is a perfect study for quiet work, warm

in winter with its log fire, and cool in summer heat.

To the left of the staircase a door goes into a roughly panelled ante-room which leads out on to the cloister, and beyond that a large stone-flagged kitchen, with offices beyond.

If you go upstairs, you find a panelled corridor with bedrooms. The one over the study is small and dark, and said to be haunted. That over the library is a big pleasant room with a fine marble fireplace — a boudoir once, I should think. Over the hall is another dark panelled room with a four-post bed, the walls hung with a most singular and rather terrible tapestry, representing a dance of death.

Beyond that, over the dining-room, is a beautiful panelled room, with a Tudor fireplace, and a bed enclosed by blue curtains. This was Hugh's own room. Out of it opens a tiny dressing-room. Beyond that is another large low room over the kitchen, which has been half-study, half-bedroom, out of which opens a little stair-

[9]

way going to some little rooms beyond
over the offices.

Above that again are some quaint white-
washed attics with dormers and leaning
walls; one or two of these are bedrooms.
One, very large and long, runs along most
of the front, and has a curious leaden
channel in it a foot above the floor to
take the rain-water off the leads of the
roof. Out of another comes a sweet smell
of stored apples, which revives the memory
of childish visits to farm storerooms —
and here stands a pretty and quaint old
pipe-organ awaiting renovation.

We must retrace our steps to the building at the back to which the cloister leads.
We enter a little sacristy and vestry, and
beyond is a dark chapel, with a side-chapel
opening out of it. It was originally an old
brew-house, with a timbered roof. The
sanctuary is now divided off by a high
open screen, of old oak, reaching nearly
to the roof. The whole place is full of
statues, carved and painted, embroidered
hangings, stained glass, pendent lamps,

emblems; there is a gallery over the sacristy, with an organ, and a fine piece of old embroidery displayed on the gallery front.

This is the house in which for seven years my brother Hugh lived. Let me recall how he first came to see it. He was at Cambridge then, working as an assistant priest. He became aware that his work lay rather in the direction of speaking, preaching, and writing, and resolved to establish himself in some quiet country retreat. One summer I visited several houses in Hertfordshire with him, but they proved unsuitable. One of these possessed an extraordinary attraction for him. It was in a bleak remote village, and it was a fine old house which had fallen from its high estate. It stood on the road and was used as a grocer's shop. It was much dilapidated, and there was little ground about it, but inside there were old frescoes and pictures, strange plaster friezes and moulded ceilings, which had once been brightly coloured. But

[11]

nothing would have made it a really attractive house, in spite of the curious beauty of its adornment.

One day I was returning alone from an excursion, and passed by what we call accident through Hare Street, the village which I have described. I caught a glimpse of the house through the iron gates, and saw that there was a board up saying it was for sale. A few days later I went there with Hugh. It was all extremely desolate, but we found a friendly caretaker who led us round. The shrubberies had grown into dense plantations, the orchard was a tangled waste of grass, the garden was covered with weeds. I remember Hugh's exclamation of regret that we had visited the place. "It is *exactly* what I want," he said, "but it is *far* too expensive. I wish I had never set eyes on it!" However, he found that it had long been unlet, and that no one would buy it. He might have had the pasture-land and the farm-buildings as well, and he afterwards regretted that he had not bought them, but his income from writing was still small. However, he offered what seems to me now an extraordinarily low sum for the house and garden; it was to his astonishment at once accepted. It was all going to ruin, and the owner was glad to get rid of it on any terms. He established himself there with great expedition, and set to work to renovate the place. At a later date he bought the adjacent cottage, and the paddock in which he built the other house, and he also purchased some outlying fields, one a charming spot on the road to Buntingford, with some fine old trees, where he had an idea of building a church.

Everything in the little domain took shape under his skilful hand and ingenious brain. He made most of the tapestries in the house with his own fingers, working with his friend Mr. Gabriel Pippet the artist. He carved much of the panelling — he was extraordinarily clever with his hands. He painted many of the pictures

[13]

which hang on the walls, he catalogued the library; he worked day after day in the garden, weeding, mowing, and planting. In all this he had the advantage of the skill, capacity, and invention of his factotum and friend, Mr. Joseph Reeman, who could turn his hand to anything and everything with equal energy and taste; and so the whole place grew and expanded in his hands, until there is hardly a detail, indoors or out-of-doors, which does not show some trace of his fancy and his touch.

There were some strange old traditions about the house; it was said to be haunted, and more than one of his guests had inexplicable experiences there. It was also said that there was a hidden treasure concealed in or about it. That treasure Hugh certainly discovered, in the delight which he took in restoring, adorning, and laying it all out. It was a source of constant joy to him in his life. And there, in the midst of it all, his body lies.

II

CHILDHOOOD

I VERY well remember the sudden appearance of Hugh in the nursery world, and being conducted into a secluded dressing-room, adjacent to the nursery, where the tiny creature lay, lost in contented dreams, in a big, white-draped, white-hooded cradle. It was just a rather pleasing and exciting event to us children, not particularly wonderful or remarkable. It was at Wellington College that he was born, in the Master's Lodge, in a sunny bedroom, in the south-east corner of the house; one of its windows looking to the south front of the college and the chapel with its slender spire; the other window looking over the garden and a waste of heather beyond, to the fir-crowned hill of Ambarrow. My father had been Headmaster for twelve years and was nearing the end of his time there; and I was myself nine years old, and shortly to go to a private school, where my elder brother Martin already was. My two sisters, Nelly and Maggie, were respectively eight and six, and my brother, Fred, was four — six in all.

And by a freak of memory I recollect, too, that at breakfast on the following morning my father — half-shyly, half-proudly, I thought — announced the fact of Hugh's birth to the boys whom he had asked in, as his custom was, to breakfast, and how they offered embarrassed congratulations, not being sure, I suppose, exactly what the right phrase was.

Then came the christening, which took place at Sandhurst Church, a mile or two away, to which we walked by the pine-clad hill of Edgebarrow and the heathery moorland known as Cock-a-Dobbie. Mr. Parsons was the clergyman — a little handsome old man, like an abbé, with a clear-cut face and thick white hair. I am afraid that the ceremony had no religious sig-

Photo by Hills & Saunders

THE MASTER'S LODGE, WELLINGTON COLLEGE, 1868

The room to the left of the porch is the study.   In the room above it Hugh was born.

nificance for me at that time, but I was deeply interested, thought it rather cruel, and was shocked at Hugh's indecorous outcry. He was called Robert, an old family name, and Hugh, in honour of St. Hugh of Lincoln, where my father was a Prebendary, and because he was born on the day before St. Hugh's Feast. And then I really remember nothing more of him for a time, except for a scene in the nursery on some wet afternoon when the baby — Robin as he was at first called — insisted on being included in some game of tents made by pinning shawls over the tops of chairs, he being then, as always, perfectly clear what his wishes were, and equally clear that they were worth attending to and carrying out.

Then I vividly recall how in 1875, when we were all returning *en famille* from a long summer holiday spent at Torquay in a pleasant house lent us in Meadfoot Bay, we all travelled together in a third-class carriage; how it fell to my lot to have the amusing of Hugh, and how difficult he was to amuse, because he wished to look out of the window the whole time, and to make remarks on everything. But at Lincoln I hardly remember anything of him at all, because I was at school with my elder brother, and only came back for the holidays; and we two had moreover a little sanctum of our own, a small sitting-room named Bec by my father, who had a taste for pleasant traditions, after Anthony Bec, the warlike Bishop of Durham, who had once been Chancellor of Lincoln. Here we arranged our collections and attended to our own concerns, hardly having anything to do with the nursery life, except to go to tea there and to play games in the evening. The one thing I do remember is that Hugh would under no circumstances and for no considerations ever consent to go into a room in the dark by himself, being extremely imaginative and nervous; and that on one occasion when he was asked what he expected to befall him, he said with a shudder and a stammer: "To fall over a mangled corpse, squish! into a pool of gore!"

When he was between four and five years old, at Lincoln, one of his godfathers, Mr. Penny, an old friend and colleague of my father's at Wellington College, came to stay at the Chancery, and brought Hugh a Bible. My mother was sitting with Mr. Penny in the drawing-room after luncheon, when Hugh, in a little black velvet suit, his flaxen hair brushed till it gleamed with radiance, his face the picture of innocence, bearing the Bible, a very image of early piety, entered the room, and going up to his godfather, said with his little stammer: "Tha-a-ank you, Godpapa, for this beautiful Bible! will you read me some of it?"

Mr. Penny beamed with delight, and took the Bible. My mother rose to leave the room, feeling almost unworthy of being present at so sacred an interview, but as she reached the door, she heard Mr. Penny say: "And what shall I read about?" "The De-e-evil!" said Hugh without the least hesitation. My mother closed the door and came back.

There was one member of our family circle for whom Hugh did undoubtedly cherish a very deep and tender affection from the time when his affections first awoke — this was for the beloved Beth, the old family nurse. Beth became nurse-maid to my grandmother, Mrs. Sidgwick, as a young girl; and the first of her nurslings, whom she tended through an attack of smallpox, catching the complaint herself, was my uncle, William Sidgwick, still alive as a vigorous octogenarian. Henry Sidgwick, Arthur Sidgwick, and my mother were all under Beth's care. Then she came on with my mother to Wellington College and nursed us all with the simplest and sweetest goodness and devotion. For Hugh, as the last of her "children," she had the tenderest love, and lavished her care, and indeed her money, on him. When we were all dispersed for a time after my father's death, Beth went to her Yorkshire relations, and

ROBERT HUGH BENSON AND BETH

AT THE CHANCERY, LINCOLN

IN 1876.   AGED 5

pined away in separation from her dear
ones. Hugh returned alone and earlier
than the rest, and Beth could bear it no
longer, but came up from Yorkshire just
to get a glimpse of Hugh at a station in
London as he passed through, had a few
words with him and a kiss, and gave him
some little presents which she thought he
might like, returning to Yorkshire tired
out but comforted. I have always thought
that little journey one of the most touching
and beautiful acts of love and service I
have ever heard of. She was nearly
eighty at the time.

In early days she watched over Hugh,
did anything and everything for him;
when he got older she used to delight to
wait on him, to pack and unpack for him,
to call him in the mornings, and secretly
to purchase clothes and toilet articles to
replace anything worn out or lost. In
later days the thought that he was coming home used to make her radiant for
days before. She used to come tapping
at my door before dinner, and sit down

for a little talk. "I know what you are thinking about, Beth!" "What is it, dear?" "Why, about Hugh, of course! You don't care for anyone else when he is coming." "No, don't say that, dear — but I *am* pleased to think that Master Hugh is coming home for a bit — I hope he won't be very tired!" And she used to smooth down her apron with her toil-worn hands and beam to herself at the prospect. He always went and sat with her for a little in the evenings, in her room full of all the old nursery treasures, and imitated her smilingly. "Nay, now, child! I've spoken, and that is enough!" he used to say, while she laughed for delight. She used to say farewell to him with tears, and wave her handkerchief at the window till the carriage was out of sight. Even in her last long illness, as she faded out of life, at over ninety years of age, she was made perfectly happy by the thought that he was in the house, and only sorry that she could not look after his things.

BETH

Beth had had but little education; she could read a little in a well-known book, but writing was always a slow and difficult business; but she used slowly to compile a little letter from time to time to Hugh, and I find the following put away among the papers of his Eton days and schoolboy correspondence:

ADDINGTON PARK,
[? *Nov.* 1887] *Tuesday.*

DEAREST, — One line to tell you I am sending your Box to-morrow Wednesday. I hope you will get it before tea-time. I know you will like something for tea, you can keep your cake for your Birthday. I shall think about you on Friday. Everybody has gone away, so I had no one to write for me. I thought you would not mind me writing to you. —Dearest love from your dear   BETH.

The dear Beth lived wholly in love and service; she loved just as she worked, endlessly and ungrudgingly; wherever Beth is, she will find service to render and children to love; and I cannot think that she has not found the way to her darling, and he to her.

III

TRURO

W E all went off again to Truro in
1877, when my father was made
Bishop. The tradition was that as the
train, leaving Lincoln, drew up after five
minutes at the first small station on the
line, perhaps Navenby, a little voice in
the corner said: "Is this Truro?" A
journey by train was for many years a
great difficulty for Hugh, as it always
made him ill, owing to the motion of the
carriage.

At Truro he becomes a much more
definite figure in my recollections. He was
a delicately made, light-haired, blue-eyed
child, looking rather angelic in a velvet
suit, and with small, neat feet, of which
he was supposed to be unduly aware. He
had at that time all sorts of odd tricks,

winkings and twitchings; and one very
aggravating habit, in walking, of putting
his feet together suddenly, stopping and
looking down at them, while he muttered
to himself the mystic formula, "Knuck,
Nunks." But one thing about him was
very distinct indeed, that he was entirely
impervious to the public opinion of the
nursery, and could neither be ridiculed
nor cajoled out of continuing to do anything he chose to do. He did not care the
least what was said, nor had he any morbid fears, as I certainly had as a child,
of being disliked or mocked at. He went
his own way, knew what he wanted to do,
and did it.

My recollections of him are mainly of
his extreme love of argument and the
adroitness with which he conducted it.
He did not intend to be put upon as the
youngest, and it was supposed that if he
was ever told to do anything, he always
replied: "Why shouldn't Fred?" He in-
vented an ingenious device which he once,
and once only, practised with success, of

goading my brother Fred by petty shafts of domestic insult into pursuing him, bent on vengeance. Hugh had prepared some small pieces of folded paper with a view to this contingency, and as Fred gave chase, Hugh flung two of his papers on the ground, being sure that Fred would stop to examine them. The ruse was quite successful, and while Fred was opening the papers, Hugh sought sanctuary in the nursery. Sometimes my sisters were deputed to do a lesson with him. My elder sister Nelly had a motherly instinct, and enjoyed a small responsibility. She would explain a rule of arithmetic to Hugh. He would assume an expression of despair: "I don't understand a word of it — you go so quick." Then it would be explained again: "Now do you understand?" "Of course I understand *that*." "Very well, do a sum." The sum would begin: "Oh, don't push me — don't come so near — I don't like having my face blown on." Presently my sister with angelic patience would show him a mistake.

"Oh, don't interfere — you make it all mixed up in my head." Then he would be let alone for a little. Then he would put the slate down with an expression of despair and resignation; if my sister took no notice he would say: "I thought Mamma told you to help me in my sums? How can I understand without having it explained to me?" It was impossible to get the last word; indeed he used to give my sister Maggie, when she taught him, what he called "Temper-tickets," at the end of the lesson; and on one occasion, when he was to repeat a Sunday collect to her, he was at last reported to my mother, as being wholly intractable. This was deeply resented; and after my sister had gone to bed, a small piece of paper was pushed in beneath her door, on which was written: "The most unhappiest Sunday I ever spent in my life. Whose fault?"

Again, when Maggie had found him extremely cross and tiresome one morning in the lessons she was taking, she discovered,

when Hugh at last escaped, a piece of
paper on the schoolroom table, on which
he had written:

> "Passionate Magey
> Toodle Ha! Ha!
> The old gose."

There was another story of how he was
asked to write out a list of the things he
wanted, with a view to a birthday that
was coming. The list ended:

> "A little compenshion goat, and
> A tiny-winy train, and
> A nice little pen."

The diminutives were evidently intended
to give the requirements a modest air. As
for "compenshion," he had asked what
some nursery animal was made of, a frac-
ture having displayed a sort of tough
fibrous plaster. He was told that it was
made of "a composition."

We used to play many rhyming games
at that time; and Hugh at the age of
eight wrote a poem about a swarm of
gnats dancing in the sun, which ended:

"And when they see their comrades laid
In thousands round the garden glade,
They know they were not really made
To live for evermore."

In one of these games, each player
wrote a question which was to be answered
by some other player in a poem; Hugh,
who had been talked to about the necessity
of overcoming some besetting sin in Lent,
wrote with perfect good faith as his question, "What is your sin for Lent?"

As a child, and always throughout his
life, he was absolutely free from any touch
of priggishness or precocious piety. He
complained once to my sister that when
he was taken out walks by his elders, he
heard about nothing but "poetry and civi-
lisation." In a friendly little memoir of
him, which I have been sent, I find the
following passage: "In his early childhood,
when reason was just beginning to ponder
over the meaning of things, he was so won
to enthusiastic admiration of the heroes
and heroines of the Catholic Church that
he decided he would probe for himself the

Catholic claims, and the child would say to the father, 'Father, if there be such a sacrament as Penance, can I go?' And the good Archbishop, being evasive in his answers, the young boy found himself emerging more and more in a woeful Nemesis of faith." It would be literally *impossible*, I think, to construct a story less characteristic both of Hugh's own attitude of mind as well as of the atmosphere of our family and household life than this!

He was always very sensitive to pain and discomfort. On one occasion, when his hair was going to be cut, he said to my mother: "Mayn't I have chloroform for it?"

And my mother has described to me a journey which she once took with him abroad when he was a small boy. He was very ill on the crossing, and they had only just time to catch the train. She had some luncheon with her, but he said that the very mention of food made him sick. She suggested that she should sit at the far end of the carriage and eat her own lunch,

while he shut his eyes; but he said that
the mere sound of crumpled paper made
him ill, and then that the very idea that
there was food in the carriage upset him;
so that my mother had to get out on the
first stop and bolt her food on the platform.

One feat of Hugh's I well remember.
Sir James McGarel Hogg, afterwards Lord
Magheramorne, was at the time member
for Truro. He was a stately and kindly
old gentleman, pale-faced and white-
bearded, with formal and dignified manners. He was lunching with us one day,
and gave his arm to my mother to conduct
her to the dining-room. Hugh, for some
reason best known to himself, selected that
day to secrete himself in the dining-room
beforehand, and burst out upon Sir James
with a wild howl, intended to create con-
sternation. Neither then nor ever was he
embarrassed by inconvenient shyness.

The Bishop's house at Truro, Lis Escop,
had been the rectory of the rich living of
Kenwyn; it was bought for the see and
added to. It was a charming house about

a mile out of Truro above a sequestered valley, with a far-off view of the little town lying among hills, with the smoke going up, and the gleaming waters of the estuary enfolded in the uplands beyond. The house had some acres of pasture-land about it and some fine trees; with a big garden and shrubberies, an orchard and a wood. We were all very happy there, save for the shadow of my eldest brother's death as a Winchester boy in 1878. I was an Eton boy myself and thus was only there in the holidays; we lived a very quiet life, with few visitors; and my recollection of the time there is one of endless games and schemes and amusements. We had writing games and drawing games, and acted little plays.

We children had a mysterious secret society, with titles and offices and ceremonies: an old alcoved arbour in the garden, with a seat running round it, and rough panelling behind, was the chapter-house of the order. There were robes and initiations and a book of proceedings.

Hugh held the undistinguished office of
Servitor, and his duties were mainly those
of a kind of acolyte. I think he somewhat
enjoyed the meetings, though the difficulty
was always to discover any purpose for
which the society existed. There were sub-
scriptions and salaries; and to his latest
day it delighted him to talk of the society,
and to point out that his salary had never
equalled his subscription.

There were three or four young clergy,
Arthur Mason, now Canon of Canterbury, G. H. Whitaker, since Canon of
Hereford, John Reeve, late Rector of Lambeth, G. H. S. Walpole, now Bishop of
Edinburgh, who had come down with my
father, and they were much in the house.
My father himself was full of energy and
hopefulness, and loved Cornwall with an almost romantic love. But in all of this Hugh
was too young to take much part. Apart
from school hours he was a quick, bright,
clever child, wanting to take his part in
everything. My brother Fred and I were
away at school, or later at the University;

and the home circle, except for the holidays,
consisted of my father and mother, my two
sisters, and Hugh. My father had been
really prostrated with grief at the death of
my eldest brother, who was a boy of quite
extraordinary promise and maturity of
mind. My father was of a deeply affectionate and at the same time anxious
disposition; he loved family life, but he
had an almost tremulous sense of his pa-
rental responsibility. I have never known
anyone in my life whose personality was
so strongly marked as my father's. He
had a superhuman activity, and cared
about everything to which he put his hand
with an intensity and an enthusiasm that
was almost overwhelming. At the same
time he was extremely sensitive; and this
affected him in a curious way. A careless
word from one of us, some tiny instance
of childish selfishness or lack of affection,
might distress him out of all proportion.
He would brood over such things, make
himself unhappy, and at the same time
feel it his duty to correct what he felt to

be a dangerous tendency. He could not think lightly of a trifle or deal with it lightly; and he would appeal, I now think, to motives more exalted than the occasion justified. A little heedless utterance would be met by him not by a half-humourous word, but by a grave and solemn remonstrance. We feared his displeasure very much, but we could never be quite sure what would provoke it. If he was in a cheerful mood, he might pass over with a laugh or an ironical word what in a sad or anxious mood would evoke an indignant and weighty censure. I was much with him at this time, and was growing to understand him better; but even so, I could hardly say that I was at ease in his presence. I did not talk of the things that were in my mind, but of the things which I thought would please him; and when he was pleased, his delight was evident and richly rewarding.

But in these days he began to have a peculiar and touching affection for Hugh, and hoped that he would prove the be-

loved companion of his age. Hugh used
to trot about with him, spudding up weeds
from the lawn. He used, when at home,
to take Hugh's Latin lessons, and threw
himself into the congenial task of teaching
with all his force and interest. Yet I have
often heard Hugh say that these lessons
were seldom free from a sense of strain.
He never knew what he might not be
expected to know or to respond to with
eager interest. My father had a habit, in
teaching, of over-emphasising minute details and nuances of words, insisting upon
derivations and tenses, packing into language a mass of suggestions and associations which could never have entered into
the mind of the writer. Language ought
to be treated sympathetically, as the not
over-precise expression of human emotion
and wonder; but my father made it of a
half-scientific, half-fanciful analysis. This
might prove suggestive and enriching to
more mature minds. But Hugh once said
to me that he used to feel day after day
like a small china mug being filled out of a

waterfall. Moreover Hugh's mind was lively and imaginative, but fitful and impatient; and the process both daunted and wearied him.

I have lately been looking through a number of letters from my father to Hugh in his schooldays. Reading between the lines, and knowing the passionate affection in the background, these are beautiful and pathetic documents. But they are overfull of advice, suggestion, criticism, anxious inquiries about work and religion, thought and character. This was all a part of the strain and tension at which my father lived. He was so absorbed in his work, found life such a tremendous business, was so deeply in earnest, that he could not relax, could not often enjoy a perfectly idle, leisurely, amused mood. Hugh himself was the exact opposite. He could work, in later days, with fierce concentration and immense energy; but he also could enjoy, almost more than anyone I have ever seen, rambling, inconsequent, easy talk, consisting of stories, arguments, and ideas just as they came into his head; this had no counterpart in my father, who was always purposeful.

But it was a happy time at Truro for Hugh. Speaking generally, I should call him in those days a quick, inventive, active-minded child, entirely unsentimental; he was fond of trying his hand at various things, but he was impatient and volatile, would never take trouble, and as a consequence never did anything well. One would never have supposed, in those early days, that he was going to be so hard a worker, and still less such a worker as he afterwards became, who perfected his gifts by such continuous, prolonged, and constantly renewed labour. I recollect his giving a little conjuring entertainment as a boy, but he had practised none of his tricks, and the result was a fiasco, which had to be covered up by lavish and undeserved applause; a little later, too, at Addington, he gave an exhibition of marionettes, which illustrated historical scenes. The puppets were dressed by Beth, our old

nurse, and my sisters, and Hugh was the
showman behind the scenes. The little
curtains were drawn up for a tableau which
was supposed to represent an episode in the
life of Thomas à Becket. Hugh's voice
enunciated, "Scene, an a-arid waste!"
Then came a silence, and then Hugh was
heard to say to his assistant in a loud,
agitated whisper, "Where is the Archbishop?" But the puppet had been mis-
laid, and he had to go on to the next
tableau. The most remarkable thing about
him was a real independence of character,
with an entire disregard of other people's
opinion. What he liked, what he felt,
what he decided, was the important thing
to him, and so long as he could get his way,
I do not think that he troubled his head
about what other people might think or
wish; he did not want to earn good opinions, nor did he care for disapproval or
approval; people in fact were to him at
that time more or less favourable channels
for him to follow his own designs, more or
less stubborn obstacles to his attaining his

wishes. He was not at all a sensitive or shrinking child. He was quite capable of holding his own, full of spirit and fearless, though quiet enough, and not in the least interfering, except when his rights were menaced.

IV

BOYHOOD

HE went to school at Clevedon, in Somersetshire, in 1882, at Walton House, then presided over by Mr. Cornish. It was a well-managed place, and the teaching was good. I suppose that all boys of an independent mind dislike the first breaking-in to the ways of the world, and the exchanging of the freedom of home for the barrack-life of school, the absence of privacy, and the sense of being continually under the magnifying-glass which school gives. It was dreadful to Hugh to have to account for himself at all times, to justify his ways and tastes, his fancies and even his appearance, to boys and masters alike. Bullying is indeed practically extinct in well-managed schools; but small boys are inquisitive, observant, extremely conventional, almost like savages in their inventiveness of prohibitions and taboos, and perfectly merciless in criticism. The instinct for power is shown by small boys in the desire to make themselves felt, which is most easily accomplished by minute ridicule. Hugh made friends there, but he never really enjoyed the life of the place. The boys who get on well at school from the first are robust, normal boys, without any inconvenient originality, who enjoy games and the good-natured rough and tumble of school life. But Hugh was not a boy of that kind; he was small, not good at games, and had plenty of private fancies and ideas of his own. He was ill at ease, and he never liked the town of straggling modern houses on the low sea-front, with the hills and ports of Wales rising shadowy across the mud-stained tide.

He was quick and clever, and had been well taught; so that in 1885 he won a scholarship at Eton, and entered college there, to my great delight, in the September of that year. I had just returned to Eton as a master, and was living with

Edward Lyttelton in a quaint, white-gabled house called Baldwin's Shore, which commanded a view of Windsor Castle, and overlooked the little, brick-parapeted, shallow pond known as Barnes' Pool, which, with the sluggish stream that feeds it, separates the college from the town, and is crossed by the main London road. It was a quaint little house, which had long ago been a boarding-house, and contained many low-ceiled, odd-shaped rooms. Hugh was Edward Lyttelton's private pupil, so that he was often in and out of the place. But I did not see very much of him. He was a small, ingenuous-looking creature in those days, light-haired and blue-eyed; and when a little later he became a steerer of one of the boats, he looked very attractive in his Fourth of June dress, as a middy, with a dirk and white duck trousers, dangling an enormous bouquet from his neck. At Eton he did very little in the way of work, and his intellect must have been much in abeyance; because so poor was his performance, that it became a matter

Photo by Elliott & Fry

THE THREE BROTHERS, 1882

E. F. Benson	A. C. Benson	R. H. Benson
at Marlborough.	at Cambridge.	at Mr. Cornish's School
Aged 15.	Aged 21.	at Clevedon. Aged 11.

of surprise among his companions that he
had ever won a scholarship at all.

I have said that I did not know very
much about Hugh at Eton; this was the
result of the fact that several of the boys
of his set were my private pupils. It was
absolutely necessary that a master in that
position should avoid any possibility of
collusion with a younger brother, whose
friends were that master's pupils. If it
had been supposed that I questioned
Hugh about my pupils and their private
lives, or if he had been thought likely to
tell me tales, we should both of us have
been branded. But as he had no wish to
confide, and indeed little enough to consult
anyone about, and as I had no wish for
sidelights, we did not talk about his
school life at all. The set of boys in which
he lived was a curious one; they were
fairly clever, but they must have been, I
gathered afterwards, quite extraordinarily
critical and quarrelsome. There was one
boy in particular, a caustic, spiteful, and
extremely mischief-making creature, who

turned the set into a series of cliques and parties. Hugh used to say afterwards that he had never known anyone in his life with such an eye for other people's weaknesses, or with such a talent for putting them in the most disagreeable light. Hugh once nearly got into serious trouble; a small boy in the set was remorselessly and disgracefully bullied; it came out, and Hugh was involved — I remember that Dr. Warre spoke to me about it with much concern — but a searching investigation revealed that Hugh had really had nothing to do with it, and the victim of the bullying spoke insistently in Hugh's favour.

Hugh describes how the facts became known in the holidays, and how my father in his extreme indignation at what he supposed to be proved, so paralysed Hugh that he had no opportunity of clearing himself. But anyone who had ever known Hugh would have felt that it was the last thing he would have done. He was tenacious enough of his own rights, and argumentative enough; but he never had the faintest touch of the savagery that amuses itself at the sight of another's sufferings. "I hate cruelty more than anything in the whole world," he wrote later; "the existence of it is the only thing which reconciles my conscience to the necessity of Hell."

Hugh speaks in his book, *The Confession of a Convert*, about the extremely negative character of his religious impressions at school. I think it is wholly accurate. Living as we did in an ecclesiastical household, and with a father who took singular delight in ceremonial and liturgical devotion, I think that religion did impress itself rather too much as a matter of solemn and dignified occupation than as a matter of feeling and conduct. It was not that my father ever forgot the latter; indeed, behind his love for symbolical worship lay a passionate and almost Puritan evangelicalism. But he did not speak easily and openly of spiritual experience. I was myself profoundly attracted as a boy by the æsthetic side of religion, and loved its solemnities with all my heart; but it was not

[47]

till I made friends with Bishop Wilkinson at the age of seventeen that I had any idea of spiritual religion and the practice of friendship with God. Certainly Hugh missed it, in spite of very loving and earnest talks and deeply touching letters from my father on the subject. I suppose that there must come for most people a spiritual awakening; and until that happens, all talk of emotional religion and the love of God is a thing submissively accepted, and simply not understood or realised as an actual thing.

Hugh was not at Eton very long — not more than three or four years. He never became in any way a typical Etonian. If I am asked to say what that is, I should say that it is the imbibing instinctively of what is eminently a fine, manly, and graceful convention. Its good side is a certain chivalrous code of courage, honour, efficiency, courtesy, and duty. Its fault is a sense of perfect rightness and self-sufficiency, an overvaluing of sport and games, an undervaluing of intellectual interests,

ROBERT HUGH BENSON

IN 1889.   AGE 17

As Steerer of the *St. George*, at Eton.

enthusiasm, ideas. It is not that the
sense of effortless superiority is to be emphasized or insisted upon — modesty entirely forbids that — but it is the sort of
feeling described ironically in the book
of Job, when the patriarch says to the
elders, "No doubt but ye are the people,
and wisdom shall die with you." It is a
tacit belief that all has been done for one
that the world can do, and that one's
standing is so assured that it need never
be even claimed or paraded.

Still less was Hugh a typical Colleger.
College at Eton, where the seventy boys
who get scholarships are boarded, is a
school within a school. The Collegers
wear gowns and surplices in public, they
have their own customs and traditions
and games. It is a small, close, clever
society, and produces a tough kind of self-
confidence, together with a devotion to a
particular tradition which is almost like a
religious initiation. Perhaps if the typical
Etonian is conscious of a certain absolute
rightness in the eyes of the world, the

typical Colleger has a sense almost of absolute righteousness, which does not need even to be endorsed by the world. The danger of both is that the process is completed at perhaps too early a date, and that the product is too consciously a finished one, needing to be enlarged and modified by contact with the world.

But Hugh did not stay at Eton long enough for this process to complete itself. He decided that he wished to compete for the Indian Civil Service; and as it was clear that he could not do this successfully at Eton, my father most reluctantly allowed him to leave.

I find among the little scraps which survive from his schoolboy days, the following note. It was written on his last night at Eton. He says: "*I write this on Thursday evening after ten. Peel keeping passage.*" "Peel" is Sidney Peel, the Speaker's son. The passages are patrolled by the Sixth Form from ten to half-past, to see that no boy leaves his room without permission. Then follows:

A COLLEGER

My feelings on leaving are —
> *Excitement.*
> *Foreboding of Wren's and fellows there.*
> *Sorrow at leaving Eton.*
> *Pride as being an old Etonian.*
> *Certain pleasure in leaving for many trivial matters.*
> *Feeling of importance.*
> *Frightful longing for India.*
> *Homesickness.*
> > ***DEAR ME!***

It was characteristic of Hugh that he should wish both to analyse his feelings on such an occasion, and to give expression to them.

V

AT WREN'S

HUGH accordingly went to Mr. Wren's coaching establishment in London, living partly at Lambeth, when my family were in town, and partly as a boarder with a clergyman. It was a time of hard work; and I really retain very few recollections of him at all at this date. I was myself very busy at Eton, and spent the holidays to a great extent in travelling and paying visits; and I think that Christmas, when we used to write, rehearse, and act a family play, was probably the only time at which I saw him.

Hugh went abroad for a short time to learn French, with a party of Indian Civil Service candidates, and no doubt forgot to write home, for I find the following characteristic letter of my father's to him:

SUNDAY WORK

Lambeth Palace, S.E., *30th June* 1889.

My dearest Hughie, — We have been rather mourning about not hearing one word from you. We *supposed* all would be right as you were a large party. But *one* word would be so easy to those who love you so, who have done all they could to enable you to follow your own line, against their own wishes and affection!

We hope at any rate you are writing to-day. And we have sent off "Pioneers and Founders," which we hope will both give you happy and interesting Sunday reading, and remind you of us.

Mr. Spiers writes that you are backward in French but getting on rather fast.

I want you now at the beginning of this cramming year to make two or three Resolutions, besides those which you know and have thought of often and practised:

1. To determine never to do any secular examination work on Sundays — to keep all reading that day as fitting "The *Lord's* Day" and the "Day of Rest."

I had a poor friend who would have

done very well at Oxford, but he would make no difference between Sunday and other days. He worked on just the same — and in the Examination *itself*, just as the goal was reached, he broke down and took no degree. The doctors said it was all owing to the continuous nervous strain. If he had taken the Sundays it would just have saved him.

Lord Selborne was once telling me of his tremendous work at one time, and he said, "I never could have done it, but that I took my Sundays. I never would work on them."

2. We have arranged for you to go over to the Holy Communion one day at Dinan. Perhaps some nice fellow will go with you — Mr. Spiers will anyhow. Tell us *which* Sunday, so that we may all be with you ἐν πνεύματι.

Last night we dined at the Speaker's to meet the Prince and Princess of Wales. It was very interesting. The Terrace of the House of Commons was lighted with electric light. A steamer went by and cheered!

ARTISTIC TEMPERAMENT

The Shah will fill London with grand
spectacles, and I suppose his coming will
have much effect on politics — perhaps on
India too.

All are well. — Ever your most loving
father,   EDW. CANTUAR.

I am going to preach at the Abbey to-
night.

Hugh failed, however, to secure a place
in the Indian Civil Service, and it was decided that he should go up to Trinity College, Cambridge, and read for classical
honours.

Up to this date I do not think that anything very conscious or definite had been
going on in Hugh's mind or heart. He
always said himself that it astonished him
on looking back to think how purely negative and undeveloped his early life had
been, and how it had been lived on entirely
superficial lines, without plans or ambitions, simply taking things as they came.

I think it was quite true that it was so;

his emotions were dormant, his powers
were dormant. I do not think he had
either great affections or great friendships.
He liked companionship and amusement,
he avoided what bored him; he had no
inclinations to evil, but neither had he any
marked inclinations to what was good.
Neither had any of his many and varied
gifts and accomplishments showed themselves. I used to think latterly that he
was one of the most gifted people I had
ever seen in all artistic ways. Whatever
he took up he seemed able to do, without
any apprenticeship or drudgery. Music,
painting, drawing, carving, designing —
he took them all up in turn; and I used
to feel that if he had devoted himself to
any one of them he could have reached a
high excellence. Even his literary gifts, so
various and admirable, showed but few
signs of their presence in the early days;
he was not in the least precocious. I
think that on the whole it was beneficial
to him that his energies all lay fallow. My
father, stern as his conception of duty was,

had a horror of applying any intellectual pressure to us. I myself must confess that I was distinctly idle and dilettante both as a boy at Eton and as a Cambridge under-graduate. But much as my father appre-ciated and applauded any little successes, I was often surprised that I was never taken to task for my poor performances in work and scholarship. The truth was that my eldest brother's death at Win-chester was supposed partly to have been due to his extraordinary intellectual and mental development, and I am sure that my father was afraid of over-stimulating our mental energies. I feel certain that what was going on in Hugh's case all the time was a keen exercise of observation. I have no doubt that his brain was re-ceiving and gaining impressions of every kind, and that his mind was not really in-active — it was only unconsciously amass-ing material. He had a very quick and delighted perception of human tempera-ment, of the looks, gestures, words, man-nerisms, habits, and oddities of human

[57]

beings. If Hugh had been born in a household professionally artistic, and had been trained in art of any kind, I think he would very likely have become an accomplished artist or musician, and probably have shown great precocity. But he was never an artist in the sense that art was a torment to him, or that he made any sacrifice of other aims to it. It was always just a part of existence to him, and of the nature of an amusement, though in so far as it represented the need of self-expression in forms of beauty, it underlay and permeated the whole of his life.

The first sign of his artistic enthusiasm awakening was during his time in London, when he conceived an intense admiration for the music and ceremony of St. Paul's. Sir George Martin, on whom my father had conferred a musical degree, was very kind to him, and allowed Hugh to frequent the organ-loft. "To me," Hugh once wrote, "music is the great reservoir of emotion from which flow out streams of salvation." But this was not only a mu-

sical devotion. I believe that he now
conceived, or rather perhaps developed,
a sense of the symbolical poetry of religious rites and ceremonies which remained
with him to the end. It is true to say that
the force and quality of ritual, as a prov-
ince of art, has been greatly neglected and
overlooked. It is not for a moment to be
regarded as a purely artistic thing; but
it most undoubtedly has an attraction
and a fascination as clear and as sharply
defined as the attraction of music, poetry,
painting or drama. All art is an attempt
to express a sense of the overwhelming
power of beauty. It is hard to say what
beauty is, but it seems to be one of the
inherent qualities of the Unknown, an
essential part of the Divine mind. In
England we are so stupid and so concrete
that we are apt to think of a musician as
one who arranges chords, and of a painter
as one who copies natural effects. It is not
really that at all. The artist is in reality
struggling with an idea, which idea is a
consciousness of an amazing and adorable

quality in things, which affects him passionately and to which he must give expression. The form which his expression takes is conditioned by the sharpness of his perception in some direction or other. To the musician, notes and intervals and vibrations are just the fairy flights and dances of forms audible to the ear; to the painter, it is a question of shapes and colours perceptible to the eye. The dramaatist sees the same beauty in the interplay of human emotion; while it may be maintained that holiness itself is a passionate perception of moral beauty, and that the saint is attracted by purity and compassion, and repelled by sin, disorder, and selfishness, in the same way as the artist is attracted and repelled by visible charm and ugliness.

Ritual has been as a rule so closely annexed to religion — though all spectacular delights and ceremonies have the same quality — that it has never been reckoned among artistic predilections. The aim of ritual is, I believe, a high poetry of which

the essence is symbolism and mystery.
The movement of forms solemnly vested,
and with a background of architecture and
music, produces an emotion quite distinct
from other artistic emotions. It is a
method, like all other arts, through which
a human being arrives at a sense of mysterious beauty, and it evokes in mystical
minds a passion to express themselves in
just that way and no other, and to celebrate thus their sense of the unknown.

But there has always been a natural
terror in the religious mind of laying too
much stress on this, or of seeming to en-
courage too much an æsthetic emotion. If
the first business of religion is to purify life,
there will always be a suspicion of idolatry about ritual, a fear of substituting a
vague desire for beauty for a practical
devotion to right conduct.

Hugh wrote to me some years later
what he felt about it all:

". . . Liturgy, to my mind, is nothing
more than a very fine and splendid art,

conveying things, to people who possess
the liturgical faculty, in an extraordinarily
dramatic and vivid way. I further believe that this is an art which has been
gradually brought nearer and nearer per-
fection by being tested and developed
through nineteen centuries, by every kind
of mind and nationality. The way in
which it does, indisputably, appeal to such
very different kinds of people, and unite
them, does, quite apart from other things,
give it a place with music and painting.

.   .   .   .

"I do frankly acknowledge Liturgy to
be no more than an art — and therefore
not in the least generally necessary to salvation; and I do not in the least "con-
demn" people who do not appreciate it.
It is only a way of presenting facts — and,
in the case of Holy Week Ceremonies,
these facts are such as those of the Passion
of Christ, the sins of men, the Resurrection and the Sovereignty of Christ."

.   .   .   .

I have laid stress upon all this, because I

believe that from this time the poetry and
beauty of ritual had a deep and increasing
fascination for Hugh. But it is a thing
about which it is so easy for the enemy to
blaspheme, to ridicule ceremonial in religion as a mere species of entertainment,
that religious minds have always been inclined to disclaim the strength of its
influence. Hugh certainly inherited this
particular perception from my father. I
should doubt if anyone ever knew so much
about religious ceremonial as he did, or
perceived so clearly the force of it. "I am
almost ashamed to seem to know so much
about these things," I have often heard
him say; and again, "I don't ever seem
able to forget the smallest detail of ritual."
My father had a very strong artistic nature — poetry, sculpture, painting, architecture, scenery, were all full of fascination
to him — for music alone of the arts he
had but little taste; and I think that it
ought to be realised that Hugh's nature
was an artistic one through and through.
He had the most lively and passionate

sensibility to the appeal of art. He had,
too, behind the outer sensitiveness, the
inner toughness of the artist. It is often
mistakenly thought that the artist is sensitive through and through. In my experience, this is not the case. The artist has
to be protected against the overwhelming
onset of emotions and perceptions by a
strong interior fortress of emotional calm
and serenity. It is certain that this was
the case with Hugh. He was not in the
least sentimental, he was not really very
emotional. He was essentially solitary
within; he attracted friendship and love
more than he gave them. I do not think
that he ever suffered very acutely through
his personal emotions. His energy of out-
put was so tremendous, his power of concentration so great, that he found a
security here from the more ravaging
emotions of the heart. Not often did he
give his heart away; he admired greatly,
he sympathised freely; but I never saw
him desolated or stricken by any bereave-
ment or loss. I used to think sometimes

that he never needed anyone. I never saw him exhibit the smallest trace of jealousy, nor did he ever desire to possess anyone's entire affection. He recognised any sign of affection generously and eagerly; but he never claimed to keep it exclusively as his own.

VI

CAMBRIDGE

HUGH went then to Trinity College, Cambridge, in 1890. He often talked to me in later days about his time there as an undergraduate. He found a number of his Eton contemporaries up there, and he had a very sociable time. A friend and contemporary of his at Trinity describes him as small, light, and boyish-looking. "He walked fast, and always appeared to be busy." He never cared much about athletics, but he was an excellent steerer. He steered the third Trinity boat all the time he was at Cambridge, and was a member of the Leander club. He was always perfectly cool, and not in the smallest degree nervous. He was, moreover, an excellent walker and mountain-climber. He once walked up to London from Cambridge; I have climbed

mountains with him, and he was very
agile, quick, surefooted, and entirely in-
trepid. Let me interpolate a little anecdote
of an accident at Pontresina, which might
have been serious. Hugh and I, with a
practised Alpine climber, Dr. Leith, left
Pontresina early one morning to climb a
rock-peak. We were in a light carriage
with a guide and porter. The young horse
which drew us, as we were rattling down
the high embanked road leading to Sama-
den, took a sharp turn to the right, where
a road branched off. He was sharply
checked by the guide, with the result that
the carriage collided with a stone post,
and we were all flung out down the
embankment, a living cataract of men,
ice-axes, haversacks, and wraps. The horse
fortunately stopped. We picked ourselves
ruefully up and resumed our places. Not
until we reached our destination did we
become aware that the whole incident had
passed in silence. Not one word of advice
or recrimination or even of surprise had
passed anyone's lips!

But Hugh's climbing was put a stop to
by a sharp attack of heart-failure on the
Piz Palù. He was with my brother Fred,
and after a long climb through heavy
snow, he collapsed and was with difficulty
carried down. He believed himself to be
on the point of death, and records in one
of his books that the prospect aroused no
emotion whatever in his mind either of fear
or excitement, only of deep curiosity.

While he was an undergraduate, he and
I had a sudden and overwhelming interest
in family history and genealogy. We went
up to Yorkshire for a few days one winter,
stayed at Pateley Bridge, Ripon, Bolton
Abbey, Ripley, and finally York. At
Pately Bridge we found the parish registers
very ancient and complete, and by the aid of
them, together with the printed register of
Fountains Abbey, we traced a family tree
back as far as to the fourteenth century,
with ever-increasing evidence of the poverty and mean condition of our ancestral
stock. We visited the houses and cradles
of the race, and from comfortable granges

ROBERT HUGH BENSON

IN 1893.   AGED 21

As an Undergraduate at Cambridge.

and farmsteads we declined, as the record
conducted us back, to hovels and huts of
quite conspicuous humility and squalor.
The thermometer fell lower and lower
every day in sympathy with our researches.
I remember a night when we slept in a
neglected assembly-room tacked on to a
country inn, on hastily improvised and
scantily covered beds, when the water
froze in the ewers; and an attempt to
walk over the moors one afternoon from
Masham into Nidderdale, when the springs
by the roadside froze into lumpy congeal-
ments, like guttering candles, and we were
obliged to turn back; and how we beguiled
a ten-mile walk to Ripon, the last train
having gone, by telling an enormous improvised story, each taking an alternate
chapter, and each leaving the knots to be
untied by the next narrator. Hugh was
very lively and ingenious in this, and proved
the most delightful of companions, though
we had to admit as we returned together
that we had ruined the romance of our
family history beyond repair.

HUGH

Hugh did very little work at Cambridge; he had given up classics, and was working at theology, with a view to taking Orders. He managed to secure a Third in the Tripos; he showed no intellectual promise whatever; he was a very lively and amusing companion and a keen debater; I think he wrote a little poetry; but he had no very pronounced tastes. I remember his pointing out to me the windows of an extremely unattractive set of ground-floor rooms in Whewell's Court as those which he had occupied till he migrated to the Bishop's Hostel, eventually moving to the Great Court. They look down Jesus Lane, and the long, sombre wall of Sidney Sussex Garden. A flagged passage runs down to the right of them, and the sitting-room is on the street. They were dark, stuffy, and extremely noisy. The windows were high up, and splashed with mud by the vehicles in the street, while it was necessary to keep them shut, because otherwise conversation was wholly inaudible. "What did you do there?" I said. "Heaven knows!" he answered. "As far as I can remember, I mostly sat up late at night and played cards!" He certainly spent a great deal of money. He had a good allowance, but he had so much exceeded it at the end of his first year, that a financial crisis followed, and my mother paid his debts for him. He had kept no accounts, and he had entertained profusely.

The following letter from my father to him refers to one of Hugh's attempts to economise. He caught a bad feverish cold at Cambridge as a result of sleeping in a damp room, and was carried off to be nursed by my uncle, Henry Sidgwick:

ADDINGTON PARK, CROYDON,
26th Jan. 1891.

DEAREST HUGHIE,— I was rather disturbed to hear that you imagined that what I said in October about not *needlessly indulging* was held by you to forbid your having a fire in your bedroom on the ground floor in the depth of such a winter as we have had!

[71]

You ought to have a fire lighted at such a season at 8 o'clock so as to warm and dry the room, and all in it, nearly every evening — and whenever the room seems damp, have a fire just lighted to go out when it will. It's not wholesome to sleep in heated rooms, but they must be dry. A *bed* slept in every night keeps so, if the room is not damp; but the room must not be damp, and when it is unoccupied for two or three days it is sure to get so.

Be sure that there is a good fire in it all day, and all your bed things, *mattress and all*, kept well before it for at *least* a *whole day before you go back from Uncle Henry's.*

How was it your bed-maker had not your room well warmed and dried, mattress dry, etc., before you went up this time? She ought to have had, and should be spoken to about it — *i.e.* unless you told her not to! in which case it would be very like having no breakfast!

It has been a horrid interruption in the beginning of term — and you'll have difficulty with the loss of time. Besides which I have no doubt you have been very uncomfortable.

But I don't understand why you should have "nothing to write about" because you have been in bed. Surely you must have accumulated all sorts of reflective and imaginative stories there.

It is most kind of Aunt Nora and Uncle Henry — give my love and thanks to both.

I grieve to say that many many more fish are found dead since the thaw melted the banks of swept snow off the sides of the ice. It is most piteous; the poor things seem to have come to the edge where the water is shallowest — there is a shoal where we generally feed the swans.

I am happy to say the goldfish seem all alive and merry. The continual dropping of fresh water has no doubt saved them — they were never hermetically sealed in like the other poor things.

Yesterday I was at Ringwould, near Dover. The farmers had been up all night saving their cattle in the stalls from the sudden floods.

Here we have not had any, though the earth is washed very much from the hills in streaks.

We are — at least I am — dreadfully sorry to go to London — though the house is very dull without "the boys."

All right about the books.— Ever your loving father,   EDW. CANTUAR.

Hugh was much taken up with experiments in hypnotism as an undergraduate, and found that he had a real power of inducing hypnotic sleep, and even of curing small ailments. He told my mother all about his experiments, and she wrote to him at once that he must either leave this off while he was at Cambridge, or that my father must be told. Hugh at once gave up his experiments, and escaped an unpleasant contretemps, as the authorities discovered what was going on, and actually, I believe, sent some of the offenders down.

THE CALL

Hugh says that he drifted into the idea of taking Orders as the line of least resistance, though when he began the study of theology he said that he had found the one subject he really cared for. But he had derived a very strong half-religious, half-artistic impression from reading John Inglesant just before he came up to Cambridge. He could long after repeat many passages by heart, and he says that a half-mystical, half-emotional devotion to the Person of Our Lord, which he derived from the book, seemed to him to focus and concentrate all his vague religious emotions. He attended the services at King's Chapel regularly, but he says that he had no real religious life, and only looked forward to being a country clergyman with a beautiful garden, an exquisite choir, and a sober bachelor existence.

It was on an evening walk at Addington with my mother that he told her of his intention to take Orders. They had gone together to evensong at a neighbouring church, Shirley, and as they came back in the dusk through the silent woods of the park, he said he believed he had received the call, and had answered, "Here am I, send me!" My mother had the words engraved on the inside of a ring, which Hugh wore for many years.

By far the closest and dearest of all the ties which bound Hugh to another was his love for my mother. Though she still lives to bless us, I may say this, that never did a mother give to her children a larger and a wiser love than she gave to us; she was our playmate and companion, but we always gave her a perfectly trustful and unquestioning obedience. Yet it was always a reasonable and critical obedience. She never exacted silent submission, but gave us her reasons readily. She never curtailed our independence, or oppressed us with a sense of over-anxiety. She never demanded confidence, but welcomed it with perfect understanding.

The result of this with Hugh was that he came to consult her about everything, about his plans, his schemes, his books, his

Photo by H. Walter Barnett, 12 Knightsbridge, S.W.

MRS. BENSON

MAY, 1910

beliefs. He read all his writings aloud to
her, and deferred much to her frankly
critical mind and her deeply human insight.
At the time when he was tending towards
Rome, she accompanied him every step of
the way, though never disguising from him
her own differences of opinion and belief.
It was due to her that he suspended his
decision, read books, consulted friends,
gave the old tradition full weight; he
never had the misery of feeling that she
was overcome by a helpless distress, because she never attempted to influence any
one of us away from any course we thought
it right to pursue. She did not conceal her
opinion, but wished Hugh to make up his
own mind, believing that everyone must do
that, and that the only chance of happiness
lies there.

There was no one in the world whom he
so regarded and admired and loved; but yet
it was not merely a tender and deferential
sentiment. He laid his mind open before
her, and it was safe to do that, because my
mother never had any wish to prevail by

sentiment or by claiming loyalty. He
knew that she would be perfectly candid
too, with love waiting behind all conflict
of opinion. And thus their relation was
the most perfect that could be imagined,
because he knew that he could speak and
act with entire freedom, while he recognised the breadth and strength of her mind,
and the insight of her love. No one can
really understand Hugh's life without a
knowledge of what my mother was to
him — an equal friend, a trusted adviser,
a candid critic, and a tender mother as
well. And even when he went his own way,
as he did about health and work, though
she foresaw only too clearly what the end
might be, and indeed what it actually was,
she always recognised that he had a right
to live as he chose and to work as he desired. She was not in the least blind to
his lesser faults of temperament, nor did
she ever construct an artificial image of
him. My family has, I have no doubt, an
unusual freedom of mutual criticism. I do
not think we have ever felt it to be disloyal

to see each other in a clear light. But I am inclined to believe that the affection which subsists without the necessity of cherishing illusions, has a solidity about it which more purely sentimental loyalties do not always possess. And I have known few relations so perfect as those between Hugh and my mother, because they were absolutely tender and chivalrous, and at the same time wholly candid, natural, and open-eyed.

It was at this time that my eldest sister died quite suddenly of diphtheria. I have told something of her life elsewhere. She had considerable artistic gifts, in music, painting, and writing. She had written a novel, and left unpublished a beautiful little book of her own experiences among the poor, called *Streets and Lanes of the City*. It was privately printed, and is full of charming humour and delicate observation, together with a real insight into vital needs. I always believe that my sister would have done a great work if she had lived. She had strong practical powers and

a very large heart. She had been drawn
more and more into social work at Lambeth, and I think would have eventually
given herself up to such work. She had a
wonderful power of establishing a special
personal relation with those whom she
loved, and I remember realising after her
death that each of her family felt that they
were in a peculiar and individual relation
to her of intimacy and confidence. She
had sent Hugh from her deathbed a special
message of love and hope; and this had
affected him very much.

We were not allowed to go back at once
to our work, Fred, Hugh, and myself, because of the possibility of infection; and
we went off to Seaford together for a few
days, where we read, walked, wrote letters,
and talked. It was a strange time; but
Hugh, I recollect, got suddenly weary of it,
and with the same decision which always
characterised him, said that he must go to
London in order to be near St. Paul's. He
went off at once and stayed with Arthur
Mason. I was struck with this at the

time; he did not think it necessary to offer any explanations or reasons. He simply said he could not stand it, quite frankly and ingenuously, and promptly disappeared.

VII

LLANDAFF

IN 1892 Hugh went to read for Orders, with Dean Vaughan, who held the Deanery of Llandaff together with the Mastership of the Temple. The Dean had been a successful Headmaster of Harrow, and for a time Vicar of Doncaster. He was an Evangelical by training and temperament. My father had a high admiration for him as a great headmaster, a profound and accomplished scholar, and most of all as a man of deep and fervent piety. I remember Vaughan's visits to Lambeth. He had the air, I used to think, rather of an old-fashioned and highly-bred country clergyman than of a headmaster and a Church dignitary. With his rather long hair, brushed back, his large, pale face, with its meek and smiling air, and his thin, clear, and deliberate

voice, he gave the impression of a much-
disciplined, self-restrained, and chastened
man. He had none of the brisk effectiveness or mundane radiance of a successful
man of affairs. But this was a superficial
view, because, if he became moved or interested, he revealed a critical incisiveness of
speech and judgment, as well as a profound and delicate humour.

He had collected about himself an in-
formal band of young men who read theology under his direction. He used to
give a daily lecture, but there was no
college or regular discipline. The men
lived in lodgings, attended the cathedral
service, arranged their own amusements
and occupations. But Vaughan had a
stimulating and magnetic effect over his
pupils, many of whom have risen to high
eminence in the Church.

They were constantly invited to meals
at the deanery, where Mrs. Vaughan,
a sister of Dean Stanley, and as brilliant,
vivacious, and witty a talker as her
brother, kept the circle entranced and

delighted by her suggestive and humorous
talk. My brother tells the story of how,
in one of the Dean's long and serious ill-
nesses, from which he eventually recovered,
Mrs. Vaughan absented herself one day
on a mysterious errand, and the Dean subsequently discovered, with intense amusement and pleasure, that she had gone to
inspect a house in which she intended to
spend her widowhood. The Dean told
the whole story in her presence to some of
the young men who were dining there, and
sympathised with her on the suspension
of her plans. I remember, too, that my
brother described to me how, in the course
of the same illness, Mrs. Vaughan, who
was greatly interested in some question
of the Higher Criticism, had gone to the
Dean's room to read to him, and had suggested that they should consider and discuss some disputed passage of the Old
Testament. The Dean gently but firmly
declined. Mrs. Vaughan coming down-
stairs, Bible in hand, found a caller in the
drawing-room who inquired after the Dean.

"I have just come from him," said Mrs. Vaughan, "and it is naturally a melancholy thought, but he seems to have entirely lost his faith. He would not let me read the Bible with him; he practically said that he had no further interest in the Bible!"

Hugh was very happy at Llandaff. He says that he began to read John Inglesant again, and explored the surrounding country to see if he could find a suitable place to set up a small community house, on the lines of Nicholas Ferrar's Little Gidding. This idea was thenceforth much in his mind. At this time his day-dream was that it should be not an ascetic order, but rather devotional and mystical. It was, I expect, mainly an æsthetic idea at present. The setting, the ceremonial, the order of the whole was prominent, with the contemplation of spiritual beauty as the central principle. The various strains which went to suggest such a scheme are easy to unravel. Hugh says frankly that marriage and domesticity always appeared

to him inconceivable, but at the same time
he was sociable, and had the strong creative desire to form and express a definite
conception of life. He had always the
artistic impulse to translate an idea into
visible and tangible shape. He had, I
think, little real pastoral impulse at this,
if indeed at any time, and his view was
individualistic. The community, in his
mind, was to exist not, I believe, for discipline or extension of thought, or even
for solidarity of action; it was rather to be
a fortress of quiet for the encouragement
of similar individual impulses. He used
to talk a good deal about his plans for
the community in these days — and it is
interesting to compare with this the fact
that I had already written a book, never
published, about a literary community on
the same sort of lines, while to go a little
further back, it may be remembered that at
one time my father and Westcott used to
entertain themselves with schemes for
what they called a *Cœnobium*, which was
to be an institution in which married

priests with their families were to lead a common life with common devotions.

But I used to be reminded, in hearing Hugh detail his plans, of the case of a friend of ours, whom I will call Lestrange, who had at one time entered a Benedictine monastery as a novice. Lestrange used to talk about himself in an engaging way in the third person, and I remember him saying that the reason why he left the monastery was "because Lestrange found that he could only be an inmate of a monastery in which Lestrange was also Abbot!" I did not feel that in Hugh's community there would be much chance of the independent expression of the individualities of his associates!

He was ordained deacon in 1894 at Addington, or rather in Croydon parish church, by my father, whose joy in admitting his beloved son to the Anglican ministry was very great indeed.

Before the ordination Hugh decided to go into solitary retreat. He took two rooms in the lodge-cottage of Burton Park, two or three miles out of Lincoln. I suppose he selected Lincoln as a scene endeared to him by childish memories.

He divided the day up for prayer, meditation, and solitary walks, and often went in to service in the cathedral. He says that he was in a state of tense excitement, and the solitude and introspection had an alarmingly depressing effect upon him. He says that the result of this was an appalling mental agony: "It seemed to me after a day or two that there was no truth in religion, that Jesus Christ was not God, that the whole of life was an empty sham, and that I was, if not the chiefest of sinners, at any rate the most monumental of fools." He went to the Advent services feeling, he says, like a soul in hell. But matters mended after that, and the ordination itself seemed to him a true consecration. He read the Gospel, and he remembered gratefully the sermon of Canon Mason, my father's beloved friend and chaplain.

VIII

THE ETON MISSION

THERE were many reasons why Hugh should begin his clerical work at Hackney Wick, though I suspect it was mainly my father's choice. It was a large, uniformly poor district, which had been adopted by Eton in about 1880 as the scene of its Mission. There were certain disadvantages attending the choice of that particular district. The real *raison d'être* of a School Mission is educative rather than philanthropic, in order to bring boys into touch with social problems, and to give them some idea that the way of the world is not the way of a prosperous and sheltered home. It is open to doubt whether it is possible to touch boys' hearts and sympathies much except by linking a School Mission on to some institution for the care of boys — an orphan school or a

training ship. Only the most sensitive are
shocked and distressed by the sight of hard
conditions of life at all, and as a rule boys
have an extraordinarily unimaginative way
of taking things as they see them, and not
thinking much or anxiously about mending
them.

In any case the one aim ought to be to
give boys a personal interest in such problems, and put them in personal touch with
them. But the Eton Mission was planted
in a district which it was very hard to
reach from Eton, so that few of the boys
were ever able to make a personal acquaintance with the hard and bare conditions of life in the crowded industrial
region which their Mission was doing so
much to help and uplift, or to realise the
urgency of the needs of a district which
most of them had never visited.

But if the Mission did not touch the
imagination of the boys, yet, on the other
hand, it became a very well-managed
parish, with ample resources to draw upon;
and it certainly attracted the services of a

number of old Etonians, who had reached
a stage of thought at which the problem
of industrial poverty became an interesting
one.

Money was poured out upon the parish;
a magnificent church was built, a clergy-
house was established, curates were sub-
sidised, clubs were established, and excellent work was done there. The vicar at
this time was a friend and contemporary
of my own at Eton, St. Clair Donaldson,
now Archbishop of Brisbane. He had
lived with us as my father's chaplain for a
time, but his mind was set on parish work
rather than administration. He knew
Hugh well, and Hugh was an Etonian
himself. Moreover, my father was glad
that Hugh should be with a trusted friend,
and so he went there. St. Clair Donaldson was a clergyman of an Evangelical
type, though the Mission had been pre-
viously conducted by a very High Church-
man, William Carter, the present Archbishop of Capetown. But now distinctive
High Church practices were given up, and

the parish was run on moderate, kindly, and sensible lines. Whether such an institution is primarily and distinctively religious may be questioned. Such work is centred rather upon friendly and helpful relations, and religion becomes one of a number of active forces, rather than the force upon which all depends. High-minded, duty-loving, transparently good and cheerful as the tone of the clergy was, it was, no doubt, tentative rather than authoritative.

Hugh's work there lay a good deal in the direction of the boys' clubs; he used to go down to the clubs, play and talk with the boys, and go out with them on Saturday afternoons to football and cricket. But he never found it a congenial occupation, and I cannot help feeling that it was rather a case of putting a very delicate and subtle instrument to do a rough sort of work. What was needed was a hearty, kindly, elder-brotherly relation, and the men who did this best were the good-natured and robust

men with a generic interest in the young,
who could set a clean-minded, wholesome,
and hearty example. But Hugh was not
of this type. His mind was full of mystical and poetical ideas of religion, and
his artistic nature was intent upon expressing them. He was successful in a
way, because he had by this time a great
charm of frankness and simplicity; he
never had the least temptation to draw
social distinctions, but he desired to find
people personally interesting. He used to
say afterwards that he did not really believe in what involved a sort of social
condescension, and, like another incisive
missioner, he thought that the giving up
a few evenings a week by wealthy and
even fashionable young men, however
good-hearted and earnest, to sharing the
amusements of the boys of a parish, was
only a very uncomfortable way of showing
the poor how the rich lived! There is no
sort of doubt about the usefulness and
kindliness of such work, and it obviously
is one of the experiments which may tend

to create social sympathy: but Hugh came
increasingly to believe that the way to
lead boys to religion was not through
social gatherings, but by creating a strong
central nucleus of Christian instruction
and worship; his heart was certainly not
in his work at this time, though there
was much that appealed to him particularly to his sense of humour, which was
always strongly developed.

There was an account he gave of a
funeral he had to conduct in the early
days of his work, where, after a large
congregation had assembled in the church,
the arrival of the coffin itself was delayed,
and he was asked to keep things going.
He gave out hymns, he read collects, he
made a short address, and still the under-
taker at the door shook his head. At last
he gave out a hymn that was not very
well known, and found that the organist
had left his post, whereupon he sang it
alone, as an unsustained solo.

He told me, too, that after preaching
written sermons, he resolved to try an

extempore one. He did so with much nervousness and hesitation. The same evening St. Clair Donaldson said to him kindly but firmly that preachers were of two kinds — the kind that could write a fairly coherent discourse and deliver it more or less impressively, and the kind that might venture, after careful preparation, to speak extempore; and that he felt bound to tell Hugh that he belonged undoubtedly to the first kind. This was curious, because Hugh afterwards became, by dint of trouble and practice, a quite remarkably distinguished and impressive preacher. Indeed, even before he left the Church of England, the late Lord Stanmore, who was an old friend of my father's, said to me that he had heard all the great Anglican preachers for many years, and that he had no hesitation in putting my brother in the very first rank.

However his time was very full; the parish was magnificently organised; besides the clubs there were meetings of all sorts, very systematic visiting, a ladies' settlement, plays acted by children, in which Hugh took a prominent part both in composing the libretto and rehearsing the performances, coaching as many as seventy children at a time.

He went to a retreat given by a Cowley Father in the course of his time at the Eton Mission, and heard Father Maturin unfold, with profound enthusiasm and inspiring eloquence, a scheme of Catholic doctrine, worship, and practice, laying especial stress on Confession. These ideas began to take shape in Hugh's mind, and he came to the conclusion that it was necessary in a place like London, and working among the harassed and ill-educated poor, to *materialise* religion — that is to say, to fit some definite form, rite, symbol, and practice to religious emotion. He thought that the bright, dignified, and stately adjuncts of worship, such as they had at the Eton Mission, were not adequate to awaken the sense of the personal and intimate relation between man and God.

In this belief he was very possibly right.

Of course the dangers of the theory are obvious. There is the ultimate danger of what can fairly be called superstition, that is to say giving to religion a magical kind of influence over the material side of life. Rites, relics, images tend to become, in irrational minds, invested with an inherent and mechanical sanctity, instead of being the symbols of grace. But it is necessary to risk something; and though the risk of what may be called a sort of idolatry is great, the risk of not arousing the sense of personal religion at all is greater still.

Hugh's ordination as a priest followed in 1895; and he then made a full confession before a clergyman.

In 1896, in October, my father, who had paid a state visit to Ireland, on his return went to stay with Mr. Gladstone at Hawarden, and died there in church on a Sunday morning.

I can never forget the events of that terrible day. I received a telegram at Eton which summoned me to Hawarden, but did not state explicitly that my father was dead. I met Hugh at Euston, who told me the fact, and I can recollect walking up and down the half-deserted station with him, in a state of deep and bewildered grief. The days which followed were so crowded with business and arrangements, that even the sight of my father's body, lying robed and still, and palely smiling, in the great library of the rectory failed to bring home to me the sense that his fiery, eager, strenuous life was over. I remember that Mr. and Mrs. Gladstone came to the church with us, and that Hugh celebrated and gave us the Communion. But the day when we travelled south with the coffin, the great pomp at Canterbury, which was attended by our present King and the present King of Norway, when we laid him to rest in a vault under the north-western tower, and the days of hurried and crowded business at Addington are still faint and dream-like to me.

My mother and sister went out to Egypt for the winter; Hugh's health broke down; he was threatened with rheumatic fever, and was ordered to go out with them. It was here that he formed a very close and intimate companionship with my sister Maggie, and came to rely much on her tender sympathy and wise advice. He never returned to the Eton Mission.

IX

KEMSING AND MIRFIELD

THE change proved very beneficial to
Hugh; but it was then, with returning health and leisure for reflection, that
he began to consider the whole question of
Anglicanism and Catholicism. He describes some of the little experiences which
turned his mind in this direction. He
became aware of the isolation and what he
calls the "provincialism" of the Anglican
Church. He saw many kinds of churches
and varieties of worship. He went on
through the Holy Land, and at Jerusalem
celebrated the Communion in the Chapel
of Abraham; at Damascus he heard with a
sort of horror of the submission of Father
Maturin to Rome. In all this his scheme
of a religious community revived. The ceremonial was to be Caroline. "We were to
wear no eucharistic vestments, but full sur-

plices and black scarves, and were to do nothing in particular."

When he returned, he went as curate to Kemsing, a village in Kent. It was decided that for the sake of his health his work must be light. The Rector, Mr. Skarratt, was a wealthy man; he had restored the church beautifully, and had organised a very dignified and careful musical service. Hugh lived with him at the vicarage, a big, comfortable house, with a succession of interesting guests. He had a very happy year, devoting much attention to preaching, and doing a great deal of work among the children, for which he had a quite singular gift. He had a simple and direct way with them, equally removed from both petting and authoritativeness. His own natural childlikeness came out — and indeed all his life he preserved the innocence, the impulsiveness, the mingled impatience and docility of a child more than any man I ever saw.

I remember a conversation I had with Hugh about this time. An offer had been

made to him, through me, of an important
country living. He said that he was extraordinarily happy at Kemsing but that he
was too comfortable — he needed more discipline. He said further that he was beginning to find that he had the power of
preaching, and that it was in this direction
rather than in the direction of pastoral
activity that his life was going to lie.

It was rather a pettish conversation. I
asked him whether he might not perhaps
find the discipline he needed in doing the
pastoral work which did not interest him,
rather than in developing his life on lines
which he preferred. I confess that it was
rather a priggish line to take; and in any
case it did not come well from me because
as a schoolmaster I think I always pursued
an individualistic line, and worked hard on
my own private basis of preferences rather
than on the established system of the
school. But I did not understand Hugh at
this date. It is always a strain to find one
whom one has always regarded as a boy,
almost as a child, holding strong and defi-

nitely matured views. I thought him self-
absorbed and wilful — as indeed he was —
but he was pursuing a true instinct and
finding his real life.

He then received an invitation to become a mission preacher, and went to consult Archbishop Temple about it. The
Archbishop told him, bluffly and decisively,
that he was far too young, and that before
he took it upon himself to preach to men
and women he ought to have more experience of their ways and hearts.

But Hugh with his usual independence
was not in the least daunted. He had an
interview with Dr. Gore, now Bishop of
Oxford, who was then Head of the House
of the Resurrection at Mirfield, and was
accepted by him as a probationer in the
Community. Hugh went to ask leave of
Archbishop Maclagan, and having failed
with one Primate succeeded with another.

The Community of the Resurrection was
established by Bishop Gore as an Anglican
house more or less on Benedictine lines. It
acquired a big house among gardens, built,

I believe, by a wealthy manufacturer. It
has since been altered and enlarged, but
Hugh drew an amusing set of sketches to
illustrate the life there, in which it appears
a rueful and rather tawdry building, of
yellow stone and blue slate, of a shallow and
falsetto Gothic, or with what may be called
Gothic sympathies. It is at Mirfield, near
Bradford, in the Calder valley; the country
round full of high chimneys, and the sky
much blurred with smoke, but the grounds
and gardens were large, and suited to a
spacious sort of retirement. From the
same pictures I gather that the house was
very bare within and decidedly unpleasing,
with no atmosphere except that of a
denuded Victorian domesticity.

Some of the Brothers were occupied in
definitely erudite work, editing liturgical,
expository, and devotional works; and for
these there was a large and learned library.
The rest were engaged in evangelistic mission work with long spaces of study and devotion, six months roughly being assigned
to outside activities, and six to Community

life. The day began early, the Hours were duly recited. There was work in the morning and after tea, with exercise in the afternoon. On Saturday a chapter was held, with public confession, made kneeling, of external breaches of the rule. Silence was kept from Compline, at ten o'clock, until the next day's midday meal; there was manual work, wood-chopping, coal-breaking, boot-cleaning and room-dusting. For a long time Hugh worked at step-cutting in the quarry near the house, which was being made into a garden. The members wore cassocks with a leather belt. They were called "Father" and the head of the house was "Senior" or "Superior."

The vows were simple, of poverty, chastity, and obedience, but were renewed annually for a period of thirteen months, accompanied by an expression of an intention, only, to remain in the community for life. As far as I remember, if a Brother had private means, he was bound to hand over his income but not his capital, while he was a member, and the copyright of all

books written during membership belonged
absolutely to the Community. Hugh wrote
the book of mystical stories, *The Light
Invisible*, at this time; it had a continuous
sale, and he used humorously to lament
the necessity of handing over the profits to
the Order, long after he had left it and
joined the Church of Rome. The Brothers
were not allowed, I think, to possess any
personal property, and received clothing
and small luxuries either as gifts, or purchased them through orders from the
Bursar. Our dear old family nurse, Beth,
to whom Hugh was as the apple of her eye,
used to make him little presents of things
that he needed — his wardrobe was always
scanty and threadbare — and would at
intervals lament his state of destitution.
"I can't bear to think of the greedy
creatures taking away all the gentlemen's
things!"

There was a chapel in the house, of a
High Anglican kind, where vestments and
incense were used, and plainsong sung.
There were about fourteen Brothers.

Hugh was obviously and delightfully happy at Mirfield. I remember well how he used to describe the pleasure of returning to it from a Mission, the silence, the simplicity of the life, the liberty underlying the order and discipline. The tone of the house was admirably friendly and kindly, without gossip, bickering or bitterness, and Hugh found himself among cheerful and sympathetic companions, with the almost childlike mirthfulness which comes of a life, strict, ascetic, united, and free from worldly cares. He spent his first two years in study mainly, and extended his probation. It illustrates the fact that he was acquainting himself strangely little with current theological thought that the cause of his delay was that he was entirely taken aback by a sermon of Dr. Gore's on the Higher Criticism. The whole idea of it was completely novel to Hugh, and upset him terribly, so that he thought he could hardly recover his balance. Neither then nor later had he the smallest sympathy with or interest in Modernism. Finally he took the vows in 1901; my mother was present. He was installed, his hand kissed by the Brethren, and he received the Communion in entire hopefulness and happiness. I was always conscious, in those days, that Hugh radiated an atmosphere of intense rapture and ecstasy about him: the only drawback was that, in his rare visits to home, he was obviously pining to be back at Mirfield.

Then his work began; and he says that refreshed and reinvigorated as they were before going on a Mission, by long, quiet, and careful preparation, they used to plunge into their work with ardent and eager enthusiasm. The actual mission work was hard. Hugh records that once after a Mission in London they spent four days in interviewing people and hearing confessions for eleven hours a day, with occasional sermons interspersed.

At times some of the Brothers went into residence at Westminster, in Dr. Gore's house — he was a Canon of the Abbey — and there Hugh preached his only sermon

in the Abbey. But he was now devoting
himself to Mission preaching, and perfect-
ing his system. He never thought very
highly of his gift of exposition. "I have a
certain facility in preaching, but not
much," he once said, adding, "I have far
more in writing." And I have heard him
say often that, if he let himself go in
preaching, his tendency was to become
vulgar. I have in my possession hundreds
of his skeleton notes. They consist of
the main points of his argument, written
out clearly and underlined, with a certain
amount of the texture indicated, sentence-
summaries, epigrammatic statements, dicta,
emphatic conclusions. He attained his
remarkable facility by persistent, continuous, and patient toil; and a glance at his
notebooks and fly-leaves would be the best
of lessons for anyone who was tempted to
depend upon fluid and easy volubility. He
used to say that, after long practice, a
sermon would fall into shape in a very few
moments; and I remember his once taking
a carefully written address of my own,

summarising and denuding it, and presenting me with a little skeleton of its essence,
which he implored me to use; though I
had not the courage to do so. He said, too,
that he believed that he could teach anyone of ordinary brain-power and choice of
language to preach extempore on these
lines in six months, if only he would
rigidly follow his method. His arguments,
in the course of his sermons, did not always
seem to me very cogent; but his applica-
tion of them was always most clear and
effective. You always knew exactly what
he was driving at, and what point he had
reached; if it was not good logic, it was
extremely effective logic, and you seemed
to run hand in hand with him. I remember a quite admirable sermon he preached
at Eton at this date — it was most simple
and moving. But at the same time the
effect largely depended upon a grace of
which he was unconscious — quaint, naïve,
and beautiful phrasing, a fine poetical
imagination, tiny word-pictures, and a
youthful and impetuous charm. His ges-

tures at that time were free and uncon-
strained, his voice resonant, appealing, and
clear.

He used to tell innumerable stories of his
sermon adventures. There was a story of
a Harvest Festival sermon near Kemsing,
in the days when he used a manuscript; he
found on arriving at the church that he
had left it behind him, and was allowed to
remain in the vestry during the service,
writing out notes on the inside of envelopes
torn open, with the stump of a pencil
which would only make marks at a certain
angle. The service proceeded with a shock-
ing rapidity, and when he got to the pulpit,
spread out his envelopes, and addressed
himself to the consideration of the blessings
of the Harvest, he found on drawing to an
end that he had only consumed about four
minutes. He went through the whole
again, slightly varying the phraseology,
and yet again repeated the performance;
only to find, on putting on his coat, that
the manuscript was in his pocket all the
time.

HUGH

He used to say that the most nervous experience in the world was to go into a street or market-place of a town where he was to hold a Mission with open-air sermons, and there, without accompaniment, and with such scanty adherents as he could muster, strike up a hymn. Bystanders would shrug their shoulders and go away smiling. Windows would be opened, figures would lean out, and presently withdraw again, slamming the casement.

Hugh was always extremely nervous before a sermon. He told me that when he was about to preach, he did not generally go in for the service, but remained in the vestry until the sermon; and that he would lie on a sofa or sit in a chair, in agonies of nervousness, with actual attacks of nausea, and even sickness at times, until he was summoned, feeling that he could not possibly get through. This left him after speaking a few words: but he also maintained that on the rare occasions when he felt quite confident and free from nervousness, the result was a failure: he said that a real anxiety as to the effect of the sermon was a necessary stimulus, and evoked a mental power which confidence was apt to leave dormant.

X

THE CHANGE

HUGH has himself traced in full detail, in his book *The Confessions of a Convert*, how he gradually became convinced that it was his duty to make his submission to the Church of Rome; and I will not repeat the story here. But I can recall very distinctly the period during which he was making up his mind. He left Mirfield in the early summer of 1903, so that when I came home for the summer holidays, he was living there. I had myself just accepted from King Edward the task of editing Queen Victoria's letters, and had resigned my Eton mastership. Hugh was then engaged in writing his book *By What Authority* with inconceivable energy and the keenest possible enjoyment. His absorption in the work was extraordinary. He was reading historical books and any books bearing on the history of the period, taking notes, transcribing. I have before me a large folio sheet of paper on which he has written very minutely hundreds of picturesque words and phrases of the time, to be worked into the book. He certainly soaked himself in the atmosphere of the time, and I imagine that the details are correct, though as he had never studied history scientifically, I expect he is right in saying that the mental atmosphere which he represented as existing in Elizabethan times was really characteristic of a later date. He said of the book: "I fear it is the kind of book which anyone acquainted with the history, manners, and customs of the Elizabethan age should find no difficulty in writing." He found many faults subsequently with the volume, but he convinced himself at the time that the Anglican post-Reformation Church had no identity or even continuity with the pre-Reformation Church.

He speaks of himself as undergoing an experience of great unhappiness and unrest.

Undoubtedly leaving the Mirfield Community was a painful severance. He valued a friendly and sympathetic atmosphere
very much, and he was going to migrate
from it into an unknown society, leaving
his friends behind, with a possibility of
suspicion, coldness, and misunderstanding.
It was naturally made worse by the fact
that all my father's best and oldest friends
were Anglicans, who by position and tradition would be likely to disapprove most
strongly of the step, and even feel it, if not
an aspersion on my father's memory, at all
events a disloyal and unfilial act — as
indeed proved to be the case. But I doubt
if these considerations weighed very much
with Hugh. He was always extremely
independent of criticism and disapproval,
and though he knew many of my father's
friends, through their visits to our house,
he had not made friends with them on his
own account — and indeed he had always
been so intent on the life he was himself
leading, that he had never been, so to
speak, one of the Nethinims of the sanc-

tuary; nor had the dependent and discipular attitude, the reverential attachment to venerable persons, been in the least congenial to him. He had always rather effaced himself in the presence of our ecclesiastical visitors, and had avoided the constraint of their dignity. Indeed, up to this time he had not much gone in search of personal relationships at all except with equals and contemporaries.

But the ignorance of the world he was about to enter upon was a more serious factor in his outlook. He knew that he would have to enter submissively and humbly an entirely strange domain, that he would have to join a chilly and even suspicious circle — for I suppose a convert to any new faith is .apt to be regarded, until he is fully known, as possibly weak, indeterminate, and fluctuating, and to be treated with compassion rather than admiration. With every desire to be sympathetic, people in conscious possession of security and certainty are naturally inclined to regard a claimant as bent on acquisition rather than as a hero eager for self-sacrifice.

Certainly Hugh's dejection, which I think was reserved for his tired moments, was not apparent. To me, indeed, he appeared in the light of one intent on a great adventure, with all the rapture of confidence and excitement about him. As my mother said, he went to the shelter of his new belief as a lover might run to the arms of his beloved. Like the soldier in the old song, he did not linger, but "gave the bridle-reins a shake." He was not either melancholy or brooding. He looked very well, he was extremely active in mind and in body.

I find the following extract from my diary of August:

"*August* 1903.— In the afternoon walked with Hugh the Paxhill round. Hugh is in very good cheerful spirits, steering in a high wind straight to Rome, writing a historical novel, full of life and jests and laughter and cheerfulness; not creeping in, under the shadow of a wall, sobbing as the old cords break; but excited, eager, jubilant, enjoying."

His room was piled with books and papers; he used to rush into meals with the glow of suspended energy, eat rapidly and with appetite — I have never seen a human being who ate so fast and with so little preference as to the nature of what he ate — then he would sit absorbed for a moment, and ask to be excused, using the old childish formula: "May I get down?" Sometimes he would come speeding out of his room, to read aloud a passage he had written to my mother, or to play a few chords on the piano. He would not as a rule join in games or walks — he went out for a short, rapid walk by himself, a little measured round, and flew back to his work. He generally, I should think, worked about eight hours a day at this time. In the evening he would play a game of cards after dinner, and would sit talking in the smoking-room, rapidly consuming cigarettes and flicking the ash off with his forefinger. He was also, I remember, very

argumentative. He said once of himself
that he was perpetually quarrelling with
his best friends. He was a most experi-
enced coat-trailer! My mother, my sister,
my brother, Miss Lucy Tait who lives with
us, and myself would find ourselves engaged in heated arguments, the disputants
breathing quickly, muttering unheeded
phrases, seeking in vain for a loophole or
a pause. It generally ended by Hugh
saying with mournful pathos that he could
not understand why everyone set on him —
that he never argued in any other circle,
and he could only entreat to be let alone.
It is true that we were accustomed to argue
questions of every kind with tenacity and
even with invective. But the fact that
these particular arguments always dealt
with the inconsistencies and difficulties of
ecclesiastical institutions revealed their ori-
gin. The fact was that at this time Hugh
was accustomed to assert with much
emphasis some extremely provocative and
controversial position. He was markedly
scornful of Anglican faults and manner-

DISCUSSION

isms, and behaved both then and later as if no Anglicans could have any real and vital belief in their principles, but must be secretly ashamed of them. Yet he was acutely sensitive himself, and resented similar comments; he used to remind me of the priest who said to Stevenson: "Your sect — for it would be doing it too much honour to call it a religion," and was then pained to be thought discourteous or inconsiderate.

Discourteous, indeed, Hugh was not. I have known few people who could argue so fiercely without personal innuendo. But, on the other hand, he was both triumphant and sarcastic. There was an occasion at a later date when he advanced some highly contestable points as assumptions, and my aunt, Mrs. Henry Sidgwick, in an agony of rationality, said to him, "But these things are surely matters of argument, Hugh?" To which Hugh replied, "Well, you see, I have the misfortune, as you regard it, of belonging to a Church which happens to know."

Here is another extract from my diary at this time:

"*August* 1903.— At dinner Hugh and I fell into a fierce argument, which became painful, mainly, I think, because of Hugh's vehemence and what I can only call violence. He reiterates his consciousness of his own stupidity in an irritating way. The point was this. He maintained that it was uncharitable to say, 'What a bad sermon So-and-so preached,' and not uncharitable to say, 'Well, it is better than the sickening stuff one generally hears'; uncharitable to say, 'What nasty soup this is!' and not uncharitable to say, 'Well, it is better than the filthy pigwash generally called soup.' I maintained that to say that, one must have particular soups in one's mind; and that it was abusing more sermons and soups, and abusing them more severely, than if one found fault with one soup or one sermon.

"But it was all no use. He was very impatient if one joined issue at any point, and said that he was interrupted. He dragged all sorts of red herrings over the course, the opinions of Roman theologians, and differences between mortal and venial sin, &c. I don't think he even tried to apprehend my point of view, but went off into a long rigmarole about distinguishing between the sin and the sinner; and said that it was the sin one ought to blame, not the sinner. I maintained that the consent of the sinner's will was of the essence of the sin, and that the consent of the will of the sinner to what was not in itself wrong was the essence of sin — *e.g.* not sinful to drink a glass of wine, but sinful if you had already had enough.

"It was rather disagreeable; but I get so used to arguing with absolute frankness with people at Eton that I forget how unpleasant it may sound to hearers — and it all subsided very quickly, like a boiling pot."

I remember, too, at a later date, that he produced some photographs of groups of, I think, Indian converts at a Roman Catholic Mission, and stated that anyone who had eyes to see could detect which of them had been baptized by the expression of their faces. It was, of course, a matter which it was impossible to bring to the test; but he would not even admit that catechumens who were just about to be baptized could share the same expression as those who actually had been baptized. This was a good instance of his provocative style. But it was always done like a game. He argued deftly, swiftly, and inconclusively, but the fault generally lay in his premisses, which were often wild assumptions; not in his subsequent argument, which was cogent, logical, and admirably quick at finding weak points in his adversary's armour At the same time he was wholly placable. No one could so banish and obliterate from his mind the impression of the harshest and fiercest arguments. The effervescence of his mind subsided as quickly as it arose. And my whole recollection of the period is that he was in a state of great mental and spiritual excitement, and that he was experiencing to the full the joys of combat and action.

While the interest of composition lasted, he remained at home, but the book was soon done. He was still using the oratory in the house for celebrations, and I believe that he occasionally helped in the services of the parish church. The last time I actually heard him preach was at the previous Christmas, when the sermon seemed to me both tired and hard, as of one whose emotions were strained by an interior strife.

Among his diversions at this time he painted, on the casement windows of the oratory, some figures of saints in water-colour. The designs were quaint, but in execution they were the least successful things he ever did; while the medium he employed was more apt to exclude light than to tinge it.

These strange figures became known in the village as "Mrs. Benson's dolls." They were far more visible from outside than from within, and they looked like fantastic puppets leaning against the panes.

What use my mother was supposed to make of them, or why she piled her dolls, tier above tier, in an upper window was never explained. Hugh was very indignant when their artistic merit was called in question, but later on he silently effaced them.

The curious intensity and limitation of Hugh's affections were never more exemplified than in his devotion to a charming collie, Roddy, belonging to my sister, the most engaging dog I have ever known. Roddy was a great truant, and went away sometimes for days and even weeks. Game is carefully preserved on the surrounding estates, and we were always afraid that Roddy, in his private hunting expeditions, might fall a victim to a conscientious keeper's gun, which, alas, was doubtless the cause of his final and deeply lamented disappearance. Hugh had a great affection for Roddy, and showed it, when he came to Tremans, by keeping Roddy constantly at his heels, having him to sleep in his room, and never allowing

him out of his sight. For the first day or
two Roddy enjoyed these attentions, but
gradually, as the visit lasted, became more
and more restive, and was for ever trying
to give Hugh the slip; moreover, as soon
as Hugh went away, Roddy always disappeared for a few days to recover his
sense of independence and liberty. I can
see Hugh now walking about in his cassock, with Roddy at his heels; then they
would join a circle on the lawn, and Roddy
would attach himself to some other member of the family for a little, but was always sternly whistled away by Hugh,
when he went back to his room. Moreover, instead of going back to the stable
to sleep snugly in the straw, which Roddy
loved best, he had to come to the smoking-
room, and then go back to sleep in a
basket chair in Hugh's bedroom. I can
remember Hugh departing at the end of
his visit, and saying to me, "I know it's
no use asking you — but do try to keep an
eye on Roddy! It makes me miserable
to think of his getting into the woods and

being shot." But he did not think much about Roddy in his absence, never asked to take Roddy to Hare Street; nor did he manifest deep emotion when he finally disappeared, nor make long lamentation for him. Hugh never wasted any time in vain regrets or unavailing pathos.

He paid visits to certain friends of my mother's to consult about his position. He did this solely out of deference to her wishes, but not, I think, with any hope that his purpose would be changed. They were, I believe, John Reeve, Rector of Lambeth, a very old and dear friend of our family, Bishop Wilkinson, and Lord Halifax. The latter stated his position clearly, that the Pope was Vicar of Christ *jure ecclesiastico* but not *jure divino*, and that it was better to remain an Anglican and promote unity so. Hugh had also a painful correspondence with John Words-worth, late Bishop of Salisbury, a very old friend of my father's. The Bishop wrote affectionately at first, but eventually became somewhat indignant, and told

Hugh plainly that a few months' work in a slum parish would clear his mind of doubt; the correspondence ended by his saying emphatically that he regarded conversion almost as a loss of sanity. No doubt it was difficult for one of immense patristic and theological learning, who was well versed in the historical aspect of the affair as well as profoundly conscious of the reality of his own episcopal commission, to enter the lists with a son of his old friend. But neither sympathy nor harshness could have affected Hugh at this time, any more than advice to return could alter the position of a man who had taken a leap and was actually flying through the air.

Hugh then went off on a long bicycle tour by himself, dressed as a layman. He visited the Carthusian Monastery of St Hugh, near West Grinstead, which I afterwards visited in his company. He spent a night or two at Chichester, where he received the Communion in the cathedral; but he was in an unhappy frame of mind, probably made more acute by solitude.

XI

THE DECISION

BY this time we all knew what was about to happen. "When a man's mind is made up," says the old Irish proverb, "his feet must set out on the way."

Just before my brother made his profession as a Brother of the Mirfield Community, he was asked by Bishop Gore whether he was in any danger of becoming a Roman Catholic. My brother said honestly, "Not so far as I can see." This was in July 1901. In September 1903 he was received into the Church of Rome. What was it which had caused the change? It is very difficult to say, and though I have carefully read my brother's book, the *Confessions of a Convert*, I find it hard to give a decisive answer. I have no intention of taking up a controversial attitude,

and indeed I am little equipped for doing
so. It is clear that my brother was, and
had for some time been, searching for
something, let us call it a certainty, which
he did not find in the Church of England.
The surprise to me is that one whose religion, I have always thought, ran upon
such personal and individualistic lines,
should not have found in Anglicanism the
very liberty he most desired. The distinguishing feature of Anglicanism is that
it allows the largest amount of personal
liberty, both as regards opinion and also
as regards the use of Catholic traditions,
which is permitted by an ecclesiastical
body in the world. The Anglican Church
claims and exercises very little authority
at all. Each individual Bishop has a considerable discretionary power, and some
allow a far wider liberty of action than
others. In all cases, divergences of doctrine and practice are dealt with by personal influence, tact, and compromise, and
force majeure is invoked as little as possible.
In the last hundred years, during which

there have been strong and active movements in various directions in the Church of England both towards Catholic doctrine and Latitudinarianism, such synodical and legal action as has been taken has generally proved to be a mistake. It is hard to justify the system logically and theoretically, but it may be said that the methods of the Church have at least been national, in the sense that they have suited the national temperament, which is independent and averse to coercive discipline. It may, I believe, be truly asserted that in England any Church which attempted any inquisition into the precise doctrine held by its lay members would lose adherents in large numbers. Of late the influence of the English Church has been mainly exerted in the cause of social reform, and her tendency is more and more to condone divergences of doctrine and opinion in the case of her ministers when they are accompanied by spiritual fervour and practical activity. The result has certainly been to pacify the intellectual revolt against religious opinion which was in full progress some forty years ago. When I myself was at the university some thirty years ago, the attitude of pronounced intellectuals against religious opinion was contemptuous and even derisive. That is not the case now. The instinct for religion is recognised as a vital part of the human mind, and though intellectual young men are apt at times to tilt against the travesty of orthodoxy which they propound for their own satisfaction, there is a far deeper and wider tolerance and even sympathy for every form of religious belief. Religion is recognised as a matter of personal preference, and the agnostic creed has lost much of its aggressive definiteness.

It appears to me that, so far as I can measure the movement of my brother's mind, when he decided first to take Orders his religion was of a mystical and æsthetic kind; and I do not think that there is any evidence that he really examined the scientific and agnostic position at all. His

heart and his sense of beauty were already
engaged, and life without religion would
have seemed an impossibility to him.
When he took Orders, his experience was
threefold. At the Eton Mission he was
confronted by an Anglicanism of a devout
and simple kind, which concentrated itself
almost entirely on the social aspect of
Christianity, on the love of God and the
brotherhood of man. The object of the
workers there was to create comradeship,
and to meet the problems of conduct which
arose by a faith in the cleansing and up-
lifting power of God. Brotherly love was
its first aim.

I do not think that Hugh had ever any
real interest in social reform, in politics,
in causes, in the institutions which aim at
the consolidation of human endeavour and
sympathy. He had no philosophic grasp
of history, nor was he a student of the
psychology of religion. His instincts were
all individualistic and personal; and indeed I believe that all his life he was an
artist in the largest sense, in the fact that

[134]

his work was the embodiment of dreams, the expression of the beauty which he constantly perceived. His ideal was in one sense a larger one than the technically artistic ideal, because it embraced the conception of moral beauty even more ardently than mere external beauty. The mystical element in him was for ever reaching out in search of some Divine essence in the world. He was not in search at any time of personal relations. He attracted more affection than he ever gave; he rejoiced in sympathy and kindred companionship as a flower rejoices in sunshine; but I think he had little taste of the baffled suffering which accompanies all deep human passion. He once wrote: "God has preserved me extraordinarily from intimacies with others. He has done this, not I. I have longed for intimacies and failed to win them." He had little of the pastoral spirit; I do not think that he yearned over unshepherded souls, or primarily desired to seek and save the lost. On the other hand he responded eagerly

to any claim made to himself for help
and guidance, and he was always eager not
to chill or disappoint people who seemed
to need him. But he found little satisfaction in his work at the Eton Mission,
and I do not think he would ever have
been at home there.

At Kemsing, on the other hand, he had
an experience of what I may fairly call the
epicureanism of religion. The influences
there were mainly æsthetic; the creation
of a circle like that at Kemsing would
have been impossible without wealth.
Beautiful worship, refined enjoyment, cultivated companionship were all lavished
upon him. But he soon tired of this,
because it was an exotic thing. It was a
little paradise of a very innocent kind,
from which all harsh and contradictory
elements had been excluded. But this
mere sipping of exquisite flavours became
to him a very objectless thing, because it
corresponded to no real need. I believe
that if at this time he had discovered his
literary gifts, and had begun seriously to

write, he might have been content to
remain under such conditions, at all events
for a time. But he had as yet no audience, and had not begun to exercise his
creative imagination. Moreover, to a nature like Hugh's, naturally temperate and
ardent, and with no gross or sensuous
fibre of any kind, there was a real craving
for the bareness and cleanness of self-
discipline and asceticism. There is a high
and noble pleasure in some natures towards the reduction and disregard of all
material claims and limitations, by which
a freedom and expansiveness of the spirit
can be won. Such self-denial gives to the
soul a freshness and buoyancy which, for
those who can pursue it, is in itself an
ecstasy of delight. And thus Hugh found
it impossible to stay in an atmosphere
which, though exquisitely refined and quiet,
yet hampered the energy of aspiration
and adventure.

And so he came to the Mirfield Community, and for a time found exactly
what he wanted. The Brotherhood did

not mainly concern itself with the organ-
isation of social reform, while it reduced
the complications of life to a spare and
rigorous simplicity. The question is, why
this life, which allowed him to apply all
his gifts and powers to the work which
still, I think, was the embodiment of his
visions, did not completely satisfy him?

I think, in the first place, that it is
probable that, though he was not conscious
of it, the discipline and the subordination
of the society did not really quite give
him enough personal freedom. He continued for a time to hanker after community life; he used to say, when he first
joined the Church of Rome, that he
thought he might end as a Carthusian,
or later on as a Benedictine. But he
spoke less and less of this as the years
went on, and latterly I believe that he
to contemplate it, except as a possibility
in case his powers of speech and writing
should fail him. I believe that he really,
though perhaps unconsciously, desired a
freer hand, and that he found that the

community life on the whole cramped his individuality. His later life was indeed a complete contrast to anything resembling community life; his constant restlessness of motion, his travels, his succession of engagements both in all parts of England as well as in Rome and America, were really, I do not doubt, more congenial to him; while his home life ultimately became only his opportunity for intense and concentrated literary work.

But beyond and above that lay the doctrinal question. He sums up what he came to believe in a few words, that the Church of Rome was "the divinely appointed centre of unity," and he felt the "absolute need of a Teaching Church to preserve and to interpret the truths of Christianity to each succeeding generation." Once convinced of this, argument mattered little. Hugh was entirely fearless, adventurous, and independent; he had no ambitions in the ordinary sense of the word; that is to say he made no frontal attack upon promotion or respect.

He was not what is called a "safe" man;
he had neither caution or prudence, nor
any regard for average opinion. I do not
think he ever gave allegiance to any personality, nor took any direct influence
from anyone. The various attempts he
made to consult people of different schools
of thought, all carefully recorded in his
Confessions, were made courteously and
deferentially; but it seems to me that
any opposition or argument that he en-
countered only added fuel to the fire, and
aroused his reason only to combat the suggestions with which he did not instinctively
agree. Indeed I believe that it was his
very isolation, his independence, his lack
of any real deference to personal authority,
which carried him into the Church of
Rome. One who knew Hugh well and
indeed loved him said to me a little bit-
terly that he had become a Roman Catholic not because his faith was strong, but
because it was weak. There was a touch
of truth in this. Hugh did with all his
heart desire to base his life upon some

impersonal unquestionable certainty; and where a more submissive mind might have reposed, as a disciple, upon the strength of a master, Hugh required to repose upon something august, age-long, overpowering, a great moving force which could not be too closely or precisely interrogated, but which was a living and breathing reality, a mass of corporate experience, in spite of the inconsistencies and irrationalities which must beset any system which has built up a logical and scientific creed in eras when neither logic nor science were fully understood.

The fundamental difference between Catholicism and Protestantism lies ultimately in the old conflict between liberty and discipline, or rather in the degree to which each is valued. The most ardent lover of liberty has to admit that his own personal inclinations cannot form a satisfactory standard of conduct. He must in certain matters subjugate his will and his inclination to the prevailing laws and principles and beliefs, and he must sacri-

fice his private aims and desires to the
common interest, even when his reason and
will may not be convinced. That is a
simple matter of compromise, and the
sacrifice is made as a matter of expediency
and duty rather than as a matter of emotion. But there are other natures to
whom it is essential to live by emotion,
and to whom it is a relief and delight to
submerge their private inclinations in some
larger national or religious emotion. We
have seen of late, in the case of Germany,
what tremendous strength is generated in
a nation which can adore a national ideal
so passionately that they can only believe
it to be a blessing to other nations to have
the chance given them, through devasta-
tion and defeat, of contributing to the
triumph of German ideals. I do not mean
that Catholicism is prepared to adopt
similarly aggressive methods. But what
Hugh did not find in Anglicanism was a
sense of united conviction, a world-policy,
a faith in ultimate triumph, all of which
he found in Catholicism. The Catholic

believes that God is on his side; the
Anglican hopes that he is on the side of
God. Among Anglicans, Hugh was fretted
by having to find out how much or how
little each believed. Among Catholics,
that can be taken for granted. They are
indeed two different qualities and types
of faith, and produce, or perhaps express,
different types of character. Hugh found
in the Roman Church the comfort of
corporate ideals and corporate beliefs;
and I frankly admit that the more we
became acquainted with Catholicism the
more did we recognise the strong and
simple core of evangelicalism within it,
the mutual help and counsel, the insistence
on reparation as the proof of penitence,
the insight into simple human needs, the
paternal indulgence combined with gentle
authoritativeness. All this is eminently
and profoundly Christian. It is not necessary here to say what the Anglican does
not find in it or at what point it seems to
become inconsistent with reason and liberty. But I desire to make it clear that

what Hugh needed was an emotional sur-
render and a sense of corporate activity,
and that his conversion was not a logical
one, but the discovery of a force with
which his spirit was in unison, and of a
system which gave him exactly the impetus
and the discipline which he required.

It is curious to note that Father Tyrrell,
whom Hugh consulted, said to him that he
could not receive officially any convert into
the Church except on terms which were
impossible to persons of reason; and this is
so far true that I do not believe that
Hugh's conversion was a process of either
intellect or reason. I believe that it was
a deep instinctive and emotional need for
a basis of thought so strong and vivid
that he need not question it. I believe he
had long been seeking for such a basis, and
that he was right to accept it, because he
did so in entire simplicity and genuineness.
My brother was not sceptical nor analytic;
he needed the repose of a large submission,
of obedience to an impersonal ideal. His
work lay in the presentment of religious

emotion, and for this he needed a definite
and specific confidence. In no other
Church, and least of all in Anglicanism,
could this be obtained. I do not mean for
a moment that Hugh accepted the Catholic
faith simply as a conscious relief; he was
convinced frankly and fully that the
Church of Christ could not be a divided
society, but must have a continuity of
doctrine and tradition. He believed that
to be the Divine plan and method. Having done this, his duty and his delight
were one. He tasted the full joy of obedience, the relief of not having to test, to
question, to decide; and thus his loyalty
was complete, because his heart was satisfied, and it was easier to him to mistrust
his reason rather than to mistrust his
heart. He had been swayed to and fro by
many interests and ardours and influences;
he had wandered far afield, and had found
no peace in symbolism uncertain of what
it symbolised, or in reason struggling to
reconcile infinite contradictions. Now he
rowed no more against the stream; he had

found no human master to serve, and now
he had found a great ancient and living
force which could bear him on. That was,
I think, the history of his spiritual change;
and of one thing I am sure, that no sur-
render was ever made so guilelessly, so
disinterestedly, and in so pure and simple
a mood.

He has told the story of his own recep-
tion very simply and impressively. He
wrote to my mother, "It has happened,"
and I see that he wrote also just before it
to me. I quote from my diary:

"*September* 9, 1903. — Also a note from
Hugh, from the Woodchester Dominican
Convent, saying that he thinks he will be
received this week, very short but affectionate. He says he won't attempt to say
all that is in his mind. I replied, saying
that I could not wish, knowing how he felt,
that he should do otherwise — and I
blessed him in a form of words."

It may be frankly said that however
much we regretted his choice, we none of
us had the slightest wish to fetter it, or

to discourage Hugh from following his true and conscientious convictions. One must recognise that the sunshine and the rain of God fall in different ways and at different times upon those who desire to find Him. I do not wholly understand in my mind how Hugh came to make the change, but Carlyle speaks truly when he says that there is one moral and spiritual law for all, which is that whatever is honestly incredible to a man that he may only at his direst peril profess or pretend to believe. And I understand in my heart that Hugh had hitherto felt like one out on the hillside, with wind and mist about him, and with whispers and voices calling out of the mist; and that here he found a fold and a comradeship such as he desired to find, and was never in any doubt again. And I am sure that he soon began to feel the tranquillity which comes from having taken, after much restlessness and anxiety, a hard course and made a painful choice.

At first, however, he was deeply conscious of the strain through which he had

passed. He wrote to me in answer to
the letter mentioned above:

Sept. 23, '03.

. . . Thank you so very much for your
letter. It was delightful to get it. I can't
tell you what happiness it has been through
everything to know that you, as well as
the others, felt as you did: and now your
letter comes to confirm it.

There is surprisingly little to say about
myself; since you ask —

I have nothing more than the deepest
possible conviction — no emotionalism or
sense of relief or anything of the kind.

As regards my plans — they too are tol-
erably vague. . . . All the first week I
was with the Dominicans — who, I imagine, will be my final destination after
two or three years.

. . . I imagine that I shall begin to read
Theology again, in view of future Ordination: and either I shall go to Rome at
the beginning of November; or possibly
to Prior Park, near Bath — a school, where

I shall teach an hour a day, and read
Theology.

. . . .

Mamma and I are meeting in London
next week. She really has been good to
me beyond all words. Her patience and
kindness have been unimaginable.

Well — this is a dreary and egotistical
letter. But you asked me to write about
myself.

. . . .

Well — I must thank you again for your
extreme kindness — I really am grateful:
though I am always dumb about such
things when I meet people.

. . . .

I remember taking a walk with Provost
Hornby at Eton at this date. My diary
says:

"*October* 1903. — We talked of Hugh.
The Provost was very kind and wise. He
said, 'Such a change is a testimony of
sincerity and earnestness'; he went on to
tell a story which Jowett told him of Dr.

Johnson, who said, when a husband and
wife of his acquaintance went over to
Rome, 'God bless them both.' At the
end of the walk he said to me, 'When you
write to your brother, remember me very
kindly to him, and give him, as a message
from me, what Johnson said.' This I
thought was beautiful — more than courteous."

I sent this message to Hugh, who was
deeply touched by it, and wrote the Provost
an affectionate and grateful letter.

Soon after this he went out to Rome to
prepare himself for the Orders which he
received nine months later. My mother
went to see him off. As the train went out
of the station, and Hugh was lost to view,
my mother turned round and saw Bishop
Wilkinson, one of our dearest friends, waiting for her. She had told him before that
Hugh was leaving by that train, and had
asked him to bear both herself and Hugh
in mind. He had not intruded on the
parting, but now he drew my mother's
hand into his arm and said, "If Hugh's

father, when he was here on earth, would
— and he would — have always wished
him to follow his conscience, how much
more in Paradise!" and then he went
away without another word.

XII

CAMBRIDGE AGAIN

HUGH went to the College of San Silvestro in Rome, and there he found many friends. He said that on first joining the Catholic Church, he felt like a lost dog; he wrote to me:

ROME, *Nov.* 26, '03.

. . . .

My own news is almost impossible to tell, as everything is simply bewildering: in about five years from now I shall know how I felt; but at present I feel nothing but discomfort; I hate foreign countries and foreign people, and am finding more every day how hopelessly insular I am: because of course, under the circumstances, this is the proper place for me to be: but it is a kind of dentist's chair.

. . . .

But he soon parted once and for all with his sense of isolation; while the splendours of Rome, the sense of history and state and world-wide dominion, profoundly impressed his imagination. He was deeply inspired, too, by the sight of simple and and unashamed piety among the common folk, which appeared to him to put the colder and more cautious religion of England to shame. Perhaps he did not allow sufficiently for the temperamental differences between the two nations, but at any rate he was comforted and reassured.

I do not know much of his doings at this time; I was hard at work at Windsor on the Queen's letters, and settling into a new life at Cambridge; but I realised that he was building up happiness fast. One little touch of his perennial humour comes back to my mind. He was describing to me some ceremony performed by a very old and absent-minded ecclesiastic, and how two priests stood behind him to see that he omitted nothing, "With the look in their eyes," said Hugh, "that you

can see in the eyes of a terrier who is
standing with ears pricked at the mouth
of a burrow, and a rabbit preparing to
bolt from within."

He came back a priest, and before long
he settled at Cambridge, living with
Monsignor Barnes at Llandaff House.
Monsignor Barnes was an old Eton contemporary and friend of my own, who
had begun by going to Woolwich as a
cadet; then he had taken orders in the
Church of England, and then had joined
the Church of Rome, and was put in
charge of the Roman Catholic undergraduates at Cambridge. Llandaff House is a
big, rather mysterious mansion in the
main street of Cambridge, opposite the
University Arms Hotel. It was built by
the famous Bishop Watson of Llandaff,
who held a professorship at Cambridge in
conjunction with his bishopric, and never
resided in his diocese at all. The front
rooms of the big, two-gabled house are
mostly shops; the back of the house re-
mains a stately little residence, with a

chapel, a garden with some fine trees, and opens on to the extensive and quiet park of Downing College.

Hugh had a room which looked out on to the street, where he did his writing. From that date my real friendship with him began, if I may use the word. Before that, the difference in our ages, and the fact that I was a very busy schoolmaster only paying occasional visits to home, had prevented our seeing very much of each other in anything like equal comradeship. But at the beginning of 1905 I went into residence at Magdalene as a Fellow, and Hugh was often in and out, while I was made very welcome at Llandaff House. Hugh had a small income of his own, and he began to supplement it by writing. His needs and tastes were all entirely simple. He seems to me, remembering him, to have looked extremely youthful in those days, smaller in some ways than he did later. He moved very rapidly; his health was good and his activity great. He made friends at several of the colleges, he

belonged to the Pitt Club, and he used
to attend meetings of an undergraduates'
debating club — the Decemviri — to which
he had himself belonged. One of the
members of that time has since told me
that he was the only older man he had ever
known who really mixed with undergraduates and debated with them on absolutely
equal terms. But indeed, so far as looks
went, though he was now thirty-four, he
might almost have been an undergraduate
himself.

We arranged always to walk together
on Sunday afternoons. As an old member
of King's College, I had a key of the garden there in the Backs, and a pass-key
of the college gates, which were locked on
Sunday during the chapel service. We
always went and walked about that beautiful garden with its winding paths, or sat
out in the bowling-green. Then we generally let ourselves into the college grounds,
and went up to the south porch of the
chapel, where we could hear the service
proceeding within. I can remember Hugh

saying, as the Psalms came to an end:
"Anglican double chants — how comfortable and delicious, and how entirely irre-
ligious!"

We talked very freely and openly of all
that was in our minds, and sometimes even
argued on religion. He used to tell me
that I was much nearer to his form of faith
than most Anglicans, and I can remember
his saying that the misery of being an
Anglican was that it was all so rational —
you had to make up your mind on every
single point. "Why not," he said, "make
it up on one point — the authority of the
Church, and have done with it?" "Because I can't be dictated to on points in
which I feel I have a right to an opinion."
"Ah, that isn't a faith!" "No, only a
faith in reason." At which he would
shrug his shoulders, and smile. Once I
remember his exhibiting very strong emotion. I had spoken of the worship of the
Virgin, and said something that seemed
to him to be in a spirit of levity. He
stopped and turned quite pale. "Ah,

don't say that!" he said; "I feel as if
you had said something cynical about
someone very dear to me, and far more
than that. Please promise not to speak of
it again."

It was in these days that I first perceived the extraordinary charm of both
mind and manner that he possessed. In
old days he had been amusing and argumentative enough, but he was often silent
and absorbed. I think his charm had
been developed by his new experiences, and
by the number of strangers he had been
brought into contact with; he had learned
an eager and winning sort of courtesy,
which grew and increased every year. On
one point we wholly and entirely agreed —
namely, in thinking rudeness of any kind
to be not a mannerism, but a deadly sin.
"I find injustice or offensiveness to myself
or anyone else," he once wrote, "the hard-
est of all things to forgive." We con-
curred in detesting the habit of licensing
oneself to speak one's mind, and the unpleasant English trait of confusing sincerity

ROBERT HUGH BENSON

IN 1907. AGED 35

with frank brutality. There is a sort of
Englishman who thinks he has a right, if
he feels cross or contemptuous, to lay bare
his mood without reference to his companion's feelings; and this seemed to us
both the ugliest of phenomena.

Hugh saw a good deal of academic society in a quiet way — Cambridge is a hospitable place. I remember the consterna-
tion which was caused by his fainting
away suddenly after a Feast at King's.
He had been wedged into a corner, in
front of a very hot fire, by a determined
talker, and suddenly collapsed. I was
fetched out to see him and found him
stretched on a form in the Hall vestibule,
being kindly cared for by the Master of a
College, who was an eminent surgeon and
a professor. Again I remember that we
entered the room together when dining
with a hospitable Master, and were intro-
duced to a guest, to his bewilderment, as
"Mr. Benson" and "Father Benson." "I
must explain," said our host, "that Father
Benson is not Mr. Benson's father!" "I

should have imagined that he might be
his son!" said the guest.

After Hugh had lived at Llandaff House
for a year he accepted a curacy at the
Roman Catholic church at Cambridge. I
do not know how this came about. A
priest can be ordained "to a bishop," in
which case he has to go where he is sent,
or "on his patrimony," which gives him a
degree of independence. Hugh had been
ordained "on his patrimony," but he was
advised to take up ministerial work. He
accordingly moved into the Catholic rectory, a big, red-brick house, with a great
cedar in front of it, which adjoins the
church. He had a large sitting-room,
looking out at the back over trees and
gardens, with a tiny bedroom adjoining.
He had now the command of more money,
and the fitting up of his rooms was a great
delight to him; he bought some fine old
oak furniture, and fitted the walls with
green hangings, above which he set the
horns of deer, which he had at various
times stalked and shot — he was always a

keen sportsman. I told him it was too
secular an ornament, but he would not
hear me.

Canon Scott, the rector, the kindest and
most hospitable of men, welcomed me to
the rectory, and I was often there; and
our Sunday walks continued. Hugh became known at once as the best preacher
in Cambridge, and great congregations
flocked to hear him. I do not think he had
much pastoral work to do; but now a com-
plication ensued. A good many undergraduates used to go to hear him, ask to
see him, discuss religious problems with
him. Moreover, before he left the Anglican
communion, Hugh had conducted a mission at Cambridge, with the result that
several of his hearers became Roman
Catholics. A certain amount of orthodox
alarm was felt and expressed at the new
and attractive religious element which his
sermons provided, and eventually repre-
sentations were made to me that I should
use my influence with Hugh that he should
leave Cambridge. This I totally declined

to do, and suggested that the right way to
meet it was to get an Anglican preacher to
Cambridge of persuasive eloquence and
force. I did eventually speak to Hugh
about it, and he was indignant. He said:
"I have not attempted, and shall not
attempt, any sort of proselytisation of
undergraduates — I do not think it fair,
or even prudent. I have never started the
subject of religion on any occasion with
any undergraduate. But I must preach
what I believe; and, of course, if undergraduates consult me, I shall tell them
what I think and why I think it." This
rule he strictly adhered to; and I do not
know of any converts that he made.

Moreover, it was at this time that
strangers, attracted by his sermons and
his books, began to consult him by letter,
and seek interviews with him. In this
relation he showed himself, I have reason
to know, extraordinarily kind, sympathetic,
and straightforward. He wrote fully and
as often as he was consulted; he saw an
ever-increasing number of inquirers. He

used to groan over the amount of time he
had to spend in letters and interviews, and
he used to say that it often happened that
the people least worth helping took up the
most time. He always gave his very best;
but the people who most vexed him were
those engaged in religious inquiry, not out
of any profound need, but simply for the
emotional luxury; and who argued round
and round in a circle for the pleasure of
being sympathised with. Hugh was very
clear and practical in his counsels, and he
was, I used to think, like a wise and even
stern physician, never influenced by sentiment. It was always interesting to discuss
a "case" with him. I do not mean that
he discussed his cases with me, but I used
to ask him how to deal with some intellectual or moral problem, and his insight
seemed to me wonderfully shrewd, sensible,
and clear. He had a masterly analysis,
and a power of seeing alternatives and
contingencies which always aroused my
admiration. He was less interested in the
personal element than in the psychological;

and I used to feel that his strength lay in dealing with a case scientifically and technically. Sometimes he had desperate, tragic, and even alarming cases to deal with; and here his fearlessness and toughness stood him in good stead. He never shrank appalled before any moral enormity. He told me once of a series of interviews he had with a man, not a Catholic, who appealed to him for help in the last extremity of moral degradation. He became aware at last that the man was insane, but he spared no pains to rescue him.

When he first began this work he had a wave of deep unhappiness; the responsibility of the priesthood so overwhelmed him that for a time, I have learned, he used to pray night after night, that he might die in his sleep, if it were possible. I saw and guessed nothing of this, but I think it was a mood of exhaustion, because he never exhibited anything but an eager and animated interest in life.

One of his pleasures while he was at Cambridge and ever after was the

writing, staging, and rehearsing of little
mystery-plays and sacred scenes for the
children of St. Mary's Convent at Cambridge and for the choir boys of Westminster Cathedral. These he thoroughly
enjoyed; he always loved the companionship of children, and had exactly the right
way with them, treating them seriously,
paternally, with a brisk authority, and
never sentimentally. They were beautiful
and moving little dramas, reverently performed. Unhappily I never saw one of
them. Even now I remember with a stab
of regret that he came to stay with me at
Cambridge for one of these, and besought
me to go with him. But I was shy and
busy, and though I could easily have
arranged to go, I did not and he went off
alone. "Can't you really manage it?" he
said. "Pray-a-do!" But I was obdurate,
and it gives me pain now to think that I
churlishly refused, though it is a false
pathos to dwell on such things, and both
foolish and wrong to credit the dead with
remembering trifling grievances.

But I do not think that his time at the
Catholic rectory was a really very happy
one. He needed more freedom; he became
gradually aware that his work lay in the
direction of writing, of lecturing, of preaching, and of advising. He took his own
measure and knew his own strength. "I
have *no* pastoral gift," he once said to me
very emphatically. "I am not the man to
prop," he once wrote; "I can kindle sometimes, but not support. People come to
me and pass on." Nor was he at ease in
the social atmosphere of Cambridge — it
seemed to him bleak, dry, complacently
intellectual, unimaginative. He felt himself
what the law describes as "a suspected
person," with vague designs on the spiritual life of the place.

At first, he was not rich enough to live
the sort of life he desired; but he began to
receive larger incomes from his books, and
to see that it would soon be in his power
to make a home for himself. It was then
that our rambles in search of possible
houses began, while at the same time he

curtailed his own personal expenditure to
the lowest limits, till his wardrobe became
conspicuous for its antiquity. This, however, he was wholly indifferent about; his
aim was to put together a sufficient sum to
buy a small house in the country, and there
to settle "for ever," as he used to say. "A
small Perpendicular chapel and a white-
washed cottage next door is what I want
just now," he wrote about this time. "It
must be in a sweet and secret place—pref-
erably in Cornwall." Or again, "I want
and mean — if it is permitted —to live in
a small cottage in the country; to say mass
and office, and to write books. I think
that is honestly my highest ideal. I hate
fuss and officialdom and backbiting — I
wish to be at peace with God and man."
This was his dream. The house at Hare
Street was the result.

XIII

HARE STREET

I HAVE no doubt at all that Hugh's seven years at Hare Street were the happiest of his life. He generally had some companion living there — Mr. Gabriel Pippet, who did much skilful designing and artistic work with and for him; Dr. Sessions, who managed his household affairs and acted as a much needed secretary; Father Watt, who was in charge of the Hormead Mission. At one time he had the care of a little boy, Ken Lindsay, which was, I think, the greatest joy he ever had. He was a most winning and affectionate child, and Hugh's love of children was very great. He taught Ken, played with him, told him stories. Among his papers are little touching trifles which testify to his love of the child — a withered flower, or some leaves in an envelope,

AT HARE STREET, 1909

Mr. J. Reeman.   Ken.   R. H. Benson.

"flower which Ken gave me," "leaves with which Ken tried to make a crown," and there are broken toys of Ken's put away, and little games and pictures which Hugh contrived for his pleasure, memories of happy days and hours. He used to talk about Ken and tell stories about his sayings and doings, and for a time Ken's presence gave a sense of home about Hare Street, and filled a part of Hugh's heart as nothing else did. It was a pleasure to see them together; Hugh's whole voice and bearing changed when Ken was with him, but he did not spoil him in the least or indulge him foolishly. I remember sitting with Hugh once when Ken was playing about, and how Hugh followed him with his eyes or listened to Ken's confidences and discoveries. But circumstances arose which made it necessary that Ken should go, and the loss of him was a great grief to Hugh— though even so, I admired the way in which he accepted the necessity. He always loved what he had got, but did not miss it if he lost it.

He made friends, too, with the people
of the village, put his chapel at their dis-
posal for daily use, and had a Christmas
festival there for them. He formed pleasant acquaintances with his country neighbours, and used to go to fish or shoot with
them, or occasionally to dine out. He
bought and restored a cottage which bor-
dered on his garden, and built another
house in a paddock beyond his orchard,
both of which were let to friends. Thus
it was not a solitary life at all.

He had in his mind for a long time a
scheme which he intended to carry out as
soon as he had more leisure,— for it must
be remembered that much of his lecturing
and occasional writing was undertaken
simply to earn money to enable him to
accomplish his purposes. This was to
found a community of like-minded people,
who desired more opportunity for quiet
devotion and meditation, for solitary work
and contemplation, than the life of the
world could afford them. Sometimes he
designed a joint establishment, sometimes

small separate houses; but the essence of it all was solitude, cheered by sympathy and enough friendly companionship to avoid morbidity. At one time he planned a boys' home, in connection with the work of his friend Mr. Norman Potter, at another a home of rest for troubled and invalided people, at another a community for poor and sensitive people, who "if they could get away from squalor and conflict, would blow like flowers." With his love of precise detail, he drew up time-tables, so many hours for devotion and meditation, so many for work and exercise, so many for sociability.

But gradually his engagements increased so that he was constantly away, preaching and lecturing; and thus he was seldom at home for more than two or three days at a time. Thrice he went to Rome to preach courses of sermons, and thrice he went to America, where he made many friends. Until latterly he used to go away for holidays of various kinds, a motor tour in France, a trip to Switzerland, where he

climbed mountains; and he often went to
stay with Lord Kenmare at Killarney,
where he stalked deer, shot and fished, and
lived an out-of-door life. I remember his
describing to me an incident on one of
those visits, how he was returning from a
deer-stalk, in the roughest clothes, when he
saw a little group of people in a by-lane,
and presently a message arrived to say
that there was a dying woman by the roadside, and could he go to her. He went in
haste, heard her confession, and gave her
absolution, while the bystanders withdrew
to a distance, that no word might be over-
heard, and stood bareheaded till the end
came.

His engagement-books, of which I have
several, show a dangerous activity; it is
difficult to see how any man could have
done so much of work involving so much
strain. But he had a clear idea in his
mind. He used to say that he did not
expect to have a long life. "Many
thanks," he wrote to a friend in 1905, in
reply to a birthday letter. "I certainly

want happy returns; but not very many."
He also said that he was prepared for a
break-down in his powers. He intended to
do his work in his own way, and as much
as he could while his strength lasted. At
the same time he was anxious to save
enough money to enable him to live
quietly on at Hare Street whatever happened. The result was that even when he
came back from his journeys the time at
Hare Street was never a rest. He worked
from morning to night at some piece of
writing, and there were very few commis-
sions for articles or books which he refused.
He said latterly, in reply to an entreaty
from his dear friend Canon Sharrock, who
helped him to die, that he would take a
holiday: "No, I never take holidays now
— they make me feel so self-conscious."

He was very careful to keep up with his
home and his family ties. He used to pay
regular visits to Tremans, my mother's
house, and was generally there at Christmas or thereabouts. Latterly he had a
Christmas festival of his own at Hare

Street, with special services in the chapel,
with games and medals for the children,
and with presents for all alike — children,
tenants, servants, neighbours, and friends.
My sister, who lately spent a Christmas
with him, says that it was more like an ideal
Christmas than anything she had ever seen,
and that he himself, full of eagerness and
kindness and laughter, was the centre and
mainspring of it all. He used to invite
himself over to Cambridge not infrequently
for a night or two; and I used to run over
for a day to Hare Street to see his improve-
ments and to look round. I remember
once going there for an afternoon and suggesting a stroll. We walked to a hamlet a
little way off, but to my surprise he did
not know the name of it, and said he had
never been there. I discovered that he
hardly ever left his own little domain, but
took all his exercise in gardening or working with his hands. He had a regular
workroom at one time in the house, where
he carved, painted, or stitched tapestries —
but it was all intent work. When he came

HARE STREET, IN THE GARDEN

JULY 1911

R. H. Benson.   Dr. F. L. Sessions.

to Cambridge for a day, he would collect
books from all parts of the house, read
them furiously, "tearing the heart out of
them" like Dr. Johnson. Everything was
done thus, at top speed. His correspondence was enormous; he seldom failed to
acknowledge a letter, and if his advice were
asked he would write at great length, quite
ungrudgingly; but his constant writing told
on his script. Ten years ago it was a very
distinctive, artistic, finely formed hand,
very much like my father's, but latterly it
grew cramped and even illegible, though it
always had a peculiar character, and,
as is often the case with very marked hand-
writings, it tended to be unconsciously imitated by his friends.

I used to wonder, in talk with him, how
he found it possible to stay about so much
in all sorts of houses, and see so many
strange people. "Oh, one gets used to it,"
he said, adding: "besides, I am quite
shameless now — I say that I must have a
room to myself where I can work and smoke,
and people are very good about that."

XIV

AUTHORSHIP

AS to Hugh's books, I will here say a
few words about them, because they
were a marked part of himself; he put
much skill and care into making them, and
took fully as much rapture away. When
he was writing a book, he was like a man
galloping across country in a fresh sunny
morning, and shouting aloud for joy. But
I do not intend to make what is called an
appreciation of them, and indeed am little
competent to do so. I do not know the
conventions of the art or the conditions of
it. "Oh, I see," said a critical friend to me
not long ago in much disgust, "you read a
novel for the ideas and the people and the
story." "What do you read it for?" I
said. "Why, to see how it is done, of
course," he replied. Personally I have
never read a book in my life to see how it

is done, and what interests me, apart from the book, is the person behind it — and that is very elementary. Moreover, I have a particular dislike of all historical novels. Fact is interesting and imagination is interesting; but I do not care for webs of imagination hung on pegs of fact. Historical novels ought to be like memoirs, and they are never in the least like memoirs; in fact they are like nothing at all, except each other.

The Light Invisible always seemed to me a beautiful book. It was in 1902 that Hugh began to write it, at Mirfield. He says that a book of stories of my own, *The Hill of Trouble*, put the idea into his head — but his stories have no resemblance to mine. Mine were archaic little romances, written in a style which a not unfriendly reviewer called "painfully kind," an epigram which always gave Hugh extreme amusement. His were modern, semi-mystical tales; he says that he personally came to dislike the book intensely from the spiritual point of view, as

being feverish and sentimental, and designed unconsciously to quicken his own
spiritual temperature. He adds that he
thought the book mischievous, as laying
stress on mystical intuition rather than
Divine authority, and because it sub-
stituted the imagination for the soul.
That is a dogmatic objection rather than
a literary objection; and I suppose he
really disliked it because it reminded him
later on of a time when he was moving
among shadows. But it was the first book
in which he spread his wings, and there
is, I think, a fresh and ingenuous beauty
about it, as of a delighted adventure
among new faculties and powers.

I believe that the most beautiful book
he ever wrote was *Richard Raynal, Solitary;*
and I know he thought so himself. Of
course it is an archaic book, and written,
as musicians say, in a *mode*. It is easier
in some ways to write a book in a style
which is not authentically one's own, and
literary imitation is not the highest art;
but *Richard Raynal* has the beauty of a

fine tapestry designed on antique lines,
yet replenished and enriched by modern
emotion, like Tennyson's *Mort d'Arthur.*
Yet I am sure there is a deep charm of
pure beauty in the book, both of thought
and handling, and I believe that he put
into it the best essence of his feeling and
imagination.

As to his historical books, I can feel their
vigour and vitality, and their deft use of
old hints and fragments. I remember once
discussing one of them with him, and saying that his description of Queen Elizabeth
seemed to me very vivid, but that it reminded me of a not very authentic picture
of that queen, in spangled crimson and
lace, which hung in the hall at Addington.
Hugh laughed, and said: "Well, I must
confess that very picture was in my
mind!"

With regard to his more modern stories
it is impossible not to be impressed by
their lightness and swiftness, their flashes
of beauty and emotion, their quick rippling
talk; but it is hard, at times, not to feel

them to be vitiated by their quite unconscious tendency to represent a point of
of view. They were once called by a
malign reviewer "the most detestable
kind of tract," and though this is what
the French call a *saugrenu* criticism, which
implies something dull, boorish, and pro-
vincial, yet it is easy to recognise what
is meant. It is not unjust to resent the
appearance of the cultivated and sensitive
Anglican, highly bred and graceful, who is
sure to turn out hard and hollow-hearted,
or the shabby, trotting, tobacco-scented
Roman Catholic priest, who is going to
emerge at a crisis as a man of inspired
dignity and solemnity. Sometimes, undoubtedly, the books are too intent upon
expunging other forms of religious life,
rather than in tracing the movements of
the soul. Probably this was inseparable
from the position Hugh had taken up, and
there was not the slightest pose, or desire
to improve the situation about his mind.
The descriptions, the lightly-touched details, the naturalness and ease of the talk

are wholly admirable. He must have been
a very swift observer, both of nature and
people, because he never gave the least
impression of observing anything. I never
saw him stop to look at a view, or go into
raptures over anything beautiful or picturesque; in society he was either silent and
absorbed, or more commonly extremely
animated and expansive. But he never
seemed to be on the look-out for any impressions at all, and still less to be record-
ing them.

I believe that all his books, with the ex-
ception, perhaps, of *Richard Raynal*, can
be called brilliant improvisations rather
than deliberate works of art. "I write
best," he once said, "when I rely most on
imagination." The time which elapsed
from his conception of an idea to the time
when the book was completed was often in-
credibly short. I remember his telling me
his first swift thought about *The Coward;*
and when I next asked him about it, the
book had gone to the publishers and he
was writing another. When he was actu-

ally engaged in writing he was oblivious
of all else, and lived in a sort of dream.
I have several sketches of books which he
made. He used to make a rough outline,
a kind of *scenario*, indicating the gradual
growth of the plot. That was done rapidly, and he always said that the moment
his characters were conceived, they began
to haunt his mind with emphatic vividness; but he wrote very fast, and a great
quantity at a time. His life got fuller and
fuller of engagements, but he would get
back to Hare Street for a day or two,
when he would write from morning to
night with a brief interval for gardening
or handicraft, and briefer intervals for
meals. He was fond of reading aloud
bits of the books, as they grew. He read
all his books aloud to my mother in MS.,
and paid careful heed to her criticisms,
particularly with reference to his female
characters, though it has been truly said
that the women in his novels are mostly
regarded either as indirect obstacles or as
direct aids to conversion.

METHODS OF WRITING

Mr. Belloc once said, very wisely and truly, that inertia was the breeding-ground of inspiration. I think, on the whole, that the total and entire absence of any species of inertia in Hugh's temperament reacted in a way unfavourably on his books. I do not think they simmered in his mind, but were projected, hot and smoking, from the fiery crucible of thought. There seems to me a breathless quality about them. Moreover I do not think that there is much trace of the subtle chemistry of mutual relations about his characters. In life, people undergo gradual modifications, and other people exert psychological effects upon them. But in Hugh's books the characters are all fiercely occupied in being themselves from start to finish; they have exhausted moods, but they have not dull or vacant moods; they are always typical and emphatic. This is really to me the most interesting thing about his books, that they are all projections of his own personality into his characters. He is behind

them all; and writing with Hugh was, like
so many things that he did, a game which
he played with all his might. I have
spoken about this elsewhere, because it
accounted for much in his life; and when
he was engaged in writing, there was always the delicious sense of the child,
furiously and absorbingly at play, about
him.

It is said that no artist is ever really
interested in another artist's work. My
brothers, Fred and Hugh, my sister and
myself would sometimes be at home together, and all writing books. Hugh
was, I think, always the first inclined to
produce his work for inspection; but we
had a tacit convention which was not
in the least unsympathetic, not to feel
bound to be particularly interested in
each other's books. My books, I felt,
bored Hugh more than his bored me; but
there was this advantage, that when we
read each other's books, as we often did,
any critical praise that we could offer was
much more appreciated than if we had

ROBERT HUGH BENSON

IN 1910. AGED 39

felt bound to proffer conventional admiration. Hugh once told me that he envied my *sostenuto;* but on another occasion, when I said I had nothing to write about, and feared I had written too many books, Hugh said: "Why not write a book about having nothing to write about?" It was good advice and I took it. I can remember his real and obvious pleasure when I once praised *Richard Raynal* to him with all my might. But though he enjoyed praise, it was always rather because it confirmed his own belief that his work was worth doing. He did not depend in the smallest degree either upon applause or sympathy. Indeed, by the time that a book was out, he had generally got another on the stocks, and did not care about the previous one at all.

Neither do I think that his books emanated from a high artistic ideal. I do not believe that he was really much interested in his craft. Rather he visualised a story very vividly, and then it seemed to him the finest fun in the world

to spin it all as rapidly as he could out of
his brain, to make it all alert with glanc-
ing life. It was all a personal confession;
his books bristle with his own dreams, his
own dilemmas, his own social relations;
and when he had once firmly realised the
Catholic attitude, it seemed to him the
one thing worth writing about.

While I write these pages I have been
dipping into *The Conventionalists*. It is
full of glow and drama, even melodrama;
but somehow it does not recall Hugh to
my mind. That seems strange to me,
but I think of him as always larger than
his books, less peremptory, more tolerant,
more impatient of strain. The book is
full of strain; but then I remember that
in the old days, when he played games,
he was a provoking and even derisive
antagonist, and did not in the least resent
his adversaries being both; and I come
back to my belief in the game, and the
excitement of the game. I do not, after
all, believe that his true nature flowed
quite equally into his books, as I think

it did into *The Light Invisible* and *Richard
Raynal*. It was a demonstration, and he
enjoyed using his skill and adroitness;
he loved to present the smouldering and
flashing of passions, the thrill and sting
of which he had never known. Saved as
he was by his temperament alike from deep
suffering and tense emotion, and from any
vital mingling either with the scum and
foam or with the stagnancy and mire of
life, the books remain as a brilliant illusion,
with much of the shifting hues and chang-
ing glimmer of his own ardent and restless
mind rippling over the surface of a depth
which is always a little mysterious as to
the secrets it actually holds.

XV

FAILING HEALTH

HUGH'S health on the whole was good up to the year 1912, though he had a troublesome ailment, long ignored, which gave him a good deal of malaise. He very much disliked being spoken to about his health, and accepted no suggestions on the subject. But he determined at the end of 1912, after enduring great pain, to have an operation, which was quite successful, but the shock of which was considerable. He came down to Tremans just before, and it was clear that he suffered greatly; but so far from dreading the operation, he anticipated it with a sense of immense relief, and after it was over, though he was long unwell, he was in the highest spirits. But he said after he came back from Rome that he felt ten years older; and I can recall his com-

AT TREMANS, HORSTED KEYNES

DECEMBER, 1913

| A. C. Benson. | R. H. Benson. | E. F. Benson. |
| Aged 51. | Aged 42. | Aged 46. |

ing down to Cambridge not long after and
induging one evening in an immense series
of yawns, for which he apologised, saying,
"I'm tired, I'm tired — not at the top, but
deep down inside, don't you know?"

But it was not until 1914 that his health
really declined. He came over to Cambridge at the beginning of August, when
the war was impending. He stayed with
me over the Sunday; he was tired and
overstrained, complained that he felt unable to fix his mind upon anything, and
he was in considerable depression about
the possibility of war. I have never seen
him so little able to throw off an anxiety;
but he dined in Hall with me on the Sunday night, met some old friends, and was
full of talk. He told me later in the evening that he was in much anxiety about
some anonymous menace which he had received. He would not enter into details,
but he spoke very gravely about it. However, later in the month, I went over with
a friend to see him at Hare Street, and
found him in cheerful spirits in spite of

[189]

everything. He had just got the place,
he said, into perfect order, and now all it
wanted was to be left alone. It was a day
of bright hot sunlight, and we lunched out
of doors near the chapel under the shade of
the yew trees. He produced a peculiar
and pleasant wine, which he had made
on the most scientific principles out of
his own grapes. We went round and
looked at everything, and he showed me
the preparation for the last adornment,
which was to be a rose garden near the
chapel. We walked into the orchard and
stood near the Calvary, little thinking
that he would be laid to rest there hardly
two months later.

The weeks passed on, and at the end of
September I went to stay near Ambleside
with some cousins, the Marshalls, in a
beautiful house called Skelwith Fold,
among lovely woodlands, with the mountains rising on every side, and a far-off
view down Langdale. Here I found Hugh
staying. He was writing some Collects
for time of war, and read many of them

aloud to me for criticism. He was also painting in oils, attempting very difficult landscapes with considerable success. They stood drying in the study, and he was much absorbed in them; he also was fishing keenly in a little trout lake near the house, and walking about with a gun. His spirits were very equable and good. But he told me that he had gone out shooting in September over some fields lent him by a neighbour, and had had to return owing to breathlessness; and he added that he suffered constantly from breathlessness and pain in the chest and arms, that he could only walk a few paces at a time, and then had to rest to recover his breath. He did not seem to be anxious about it, but he went down one morning to celebrate Mass at Ambleside, refusing the offer of the car, and found himself in such pain that he then and there went to a doctor, who said that he believed it to be indigestion.

He sat that morning after breakfast with me, smoking, and complaining that

the pain was very severe. But he did
not look ill; and the pain suddenly left
him. "Oh what bliss!" he said. "It's
gone, suddenly and entirely — and now
I must go out and finish my sketch."

The only two things that made me feel
anxious were that he had given up smoking
to a considerable extent, and that he said he
meant to consult our family doctor; but
he was so lively and animated — I remember one night the immense zest and intensity with which he played a game of
throwing an old pack of cards across the
room into the grate — that it was
impossible to think that his condition was
serious.

Indeed, I said good-bye to him when he
went off, without the least anticipation of
evil. My real hope was that he would be
told he had been overdoing it, and ordered
to rest; and a few days later, when I
heard that this was what the doctor advised, I wrote to him suggesting that he
should come and settle at Cambridge for a
couple of months, do exactly what he

liked, and see as much or as little of people
as he liked. It seems that he showed this
letter to one of the priests at Manchester,
and said, "There, that is what I call a real
invitation — that is what I shall do!"

Dr. Ross-Todd saw him, and told him
that it was a neuralgic affection, "false
angina," and that his heart was sound, but
that he must diminish his work. He
pleaded to be allowed to finish his imminent
engagements; the doctor said that he
might do that, if he would put off all subsequent ones. This was wisely done, in
order to reassure him, as he was an excitable though not a timid patient. He was
at Hare Street for a day or two, and his
trusted servant, Mr. Reeman, tells me that
he seemed ill and out of spirits. The last
words he said as he drove away, looking
round the lime-encircled lawn, were, "Ah!
the leaves will all be gone when I come
home again."

He preached at Salford on October 4, and
went to Ulverston on October 5, where he
conducted a mission. On October 10 he

returned, and Canon Sharrock says that he arrived in great pain, and had to move very slowly. But he preached again on October 11, though he used none of the familiar gestures, but stood still in the pulpit. He suffered much after the sermon, and rested long in a chair in the sacristy. He started to go to London on the Monday morning, but had to return in the taxi, feeling too ill to travel. Then followed days of acute pain, during which he no doubt caught a severe chill. He could not sleep, and he could only obtain relief by standing up. He wandered restlessly one night about the corridors, very lightly clad, and even went out into the court. He stood for two or three hours leaning on the mantelpiece of his room, with Father Gorman sitting near him, and trying in vain to persuade him to retire to bed.

When he was not suffering he was full of life, and even of gaiety. He went one of these afternoons, at his own suggestion, to a cinema show with one of the priests, but though he enjoyed it, and even laughed heartily, he said later that it had exhausted him.

He wrote some letters, putting off many of his autumn and winter engagements. But he grew worse; a specialist was called in, and, though the diagnosis was entirely confirmed, it was found that pneumonia had set in.

XVI

THE END

I HAD spent a long day in London at a business meeting, where we discussed a complicated educational problem. I came away alone; I was anxious to have news of my sister, who had that morning undergone a slight operation; but I was not gravely disquieted, because no serious complications were expected.

When I reached my house there were two telegrams awaiting me, one to say that the operation had gone well, the other from Canon Sharrock, of Salford, to say that my brother was dangerously ill of pneumonia. I wired at once for a further report, and before it arrived made up my mind that I must go to him. I waited till the reply came — it was a little more favourable — went up to London, and caught a midnight train for Manchester.

MANCHESTER

The news had the effect which a sudden shock is apt to have, of inducing a sense of curious unreality. I neither read nor slept, nor even thought coherently. I was just aware of disaster and fear. I was alone in my compartment. Sometimes we passed through great, silent, deserted stations, or stopped outside a junction for an express to pass. At one or two places there was a crowd of people, seeing off a party of soldiers, with songs and cheers. Further north I was aware at one time that the train was labouring up a long incline, and I had a faint sense of relief when suddenly the strain relaxed, and the train began to run swiftly and smoothly downwards; I had just one thought, the desire to reach my brother, and over and over again the dread of what I might hear.

It was still dark and chilly when I arrived at Manchester. The great station was nearly empty. I drove hurriedly through dimly-lit streets. Sometimes great factories towered up, or dark house-fronts shuttered close. Here there were high steel

networks of viaducts overhead, or parapets
of bridges over hidden waterways. At last
I came to where a great church towered up,
and an iron-studded door in a blank wall
appeared. I was told this was the place,
and pushing it open I went up a stone-
flagged path, among beds of soot-stained
shrubs, to where a lantern shone in the
porch of a sombre house. There was a
window high up on the left, where a
shaded lamp was burning and a fire flick-
ered on the ceiling, and I knew instinctively that this was my brother's room. I
rang, and presently a weary-eyed, kindly
priest, in a hastily-donned cassock, appeared. He said at once that my brother
was a little better and was asleep. The
doctors were to see him at nine. I asked
where I could go, and he advised a hotel
hard by. "We did not expect you," he
said, "or we would have had a room
ready, but now I fear we could hardly
make you comfortable."

I went to the hotel, a big, well-equipped
place, and was taken to a bedroom, where

LAST ILLNESS

I slept profoundly, out of utter weariness.
Then I went down to the Bishop's House
again at nine o'clock. By daylight Manchester had a grim and sinister air. It was
raining softly and the air was heavy with
smoke. The Bishop's House stood in what
was evidently a poor quarter, full of mean
houses and factories, all of red brick,
smeared and stained with soot. The house
itself appeared like a great college, with
paved corridors, dark arches, and many
doors. There was a lighted room like a
sacristy, and a faint scent of incense drifted
in from the door which led into the church.
Upstairs, in a huge throne-room with a
gilded chair of state and long, bare tables,
I met the doctors — Dr. Bradley, a Catholic, and Professor Murray, a famous Manchester physician, in khaki uniform, both
most gentle and kind. Canon Sharrock
joined us, a tall, robust man, with a
beautiful tenderness of manner and a
brotherly air. They gave me a better
report, but could not disguise from me
that things were very critical. It was

pneumonia of a very grave kind which had supervened on a condition of overwork and exhaustion. I see now that they had very little hope of recovery, but I did not wholly perceive it then.

Then I went with the Canon to the end of the room. I saw two iron cylinders on the table with brass fittings, and somehow knew that they contained oxygen.

The Canon knocked, and Hugh's voice said, clearly and resonantly, "Come in." I found him in bed, in a big library, the Bishop's own room. There were few signs of illness except a steam-kettle and a few bottles; a nurse was in the adjoining room. He was unable to speak very much, as his throat troubled him; but he was full of humour and brightness. I told him such news as I could think of. He knew that I was very busy, but was pleased that I had come to see him. He said that he felt really better, and that I should be able to go back the next day. He said a few words about a will he had made, but added, "Mind, I don't think I am going to die! I

BISHOP'S HOUSE, SALFORD

The Church on the left is the transept of St. John's Cathedral, Salford, where Hugh preached his last sermon. The room in which he died was the Bishop's Library. One of its windows is visible on the first floor to the left of the porch.

did yesterday, but I feel really better. This is only by way of precaution." We talked about a friend of mine in Manchester, a militant Protestant. "Yes," said Hugh, "he spoke of me the other day as a 'hell-hound'— not very tactful!" He said that he could not sleep for long together, but that he did not feel tired — only bored. I was told I must not stay long with him. He said once or twice, "It's awfully good of you to have come."

I went away after a little, feeling very much reassured. He did not give the impression of being gravely ill at all, he was so entirely himself. I wrote a few letters and then returned, while he ate his luncheon, a baked apple — but this was painful to him and he soon desisted. He talked again a little, with the same liveliness, but as he began to be drowsy, I left him again.

Dr. Bradley soon came to me, and confessed he felt anxious. "It may be a long and critical business," he said. "If he can maintain his strength like this for several days, he may turn the corner — he is a difficult patient. He is not afraid, but he is excitable, and is always asking for relief and suggesting remedies." I said something about summoning the others. "On no account," he said. "It would give him the one impression we must try to avoid — much depends upon his own hopefulness."

I went back to my hotel, slumbered over a book, went in for a little to the cathedral service, and came back about five o'clock. The nurse was not in the room at the moment. Hugh said a few words to me, but had a sudden attack of faintness. I gave him a little whisky at his own request, the doctor was fetched, and there followed a very anxious hour, while various remedies were tried, and eventually oxygen revived him. He laid his head down on the pillow, smiled at me, and said, "Oh, what bliss! I feel absolutely comfortable — it's wonderful."

The doctor beckoned me out, and told me that I had better move my things across to the house and sleep there. "I don't like the look of things at all," he said; "your place is certainly here." He added that we had better wait until the morning before deciding whether the others should be sent for. I moved my things in, and had supper with the priests, who were very kind to me. They talked much about Hugh, of his gaiety and humour; and I saw that he had given his best to these friends of his, and lived with them in brotherly simplicity.

I did not then think he was going to die, and I certainly expected no sudden change. I ought, no doubt, to have realised that the doctors had done their best to prepare me for his death; but the mind has an instinctive way of holding out the shield of hope against such fears.

I was told at this time that he to was be left quiet, so I merely slipped in at ten o'clock. Hugh was drowsy and resting quietly; he just gave me a nod and a smile.

The one thing which made me anxious, on thinking over our interviews in the course of the day was this — that he

seemed to have a preoccupation in his
mind, though he had spoken cheerfully
enough about various matters. It did not
seem either a fear or an anxiety. It was
rather that he knew that he might die, I
now believe, and that he desired to live,
and was thinking about all the things he
had to do and wished to do, and that his
trains of thought continually ended in the
thought —"Perhaps I may not live to do
them." He wished too, I thought, to reassure himself, and was pleased at feeling
better, and at seeing that I thought him
better than I had expected. He was a
sensitive patient, the doctor said, and often
suggested means of keeping up his strength.
But he showed no fear at any time,
though he seemed like one who was facing
a foe; like a soldier in the trenches with
an enemy opposite him whom he could
not quite discern.

However, I went off to bed, feeling suddenly very tired — I had been for thirty-
six hours almost without sleep, and it
seemed to me as if whole days had passed

since I left Cambridge. My room was far
away, a little plain cell in a distant corridor
high up. I slept a little; when suddenly,
through the glass window above my door,
I saw the gleam of a light, and became
aware that someone was rapidly drawing
near in the corridor. In a moment Canon
Sharrock tapped and entered. He said:
"Mr. Benson, your brother is sinking fast
— he has asked for you; he said, 'Is my
brother anywhere near at hand?' and when
I said yes, that you were in the house, he
said, 'Thank God!' Do not lose any time;
I will leave the nurse on the stairs to light
you." He went out, and I put on a few
things and went down the great dark
arches of the staircase, with a glimmering
light below, and through the throne-room
with the nurse. When I came in I saw
Hugh sitting up in bed; they had put a
chair beside him, covered with cushions,
for him to lean against. He was pale and
breathing very fast, with the nurse spong-
ing his brow. Canon Sharrock was standing at the foot of the bed, with his stole on,

reading the last prayers from a little book.
When I entered, Hugh fixed his eyes on me
with a strange smile, with something triumphant in it, and said in a clear, natural
voice, "Arthur, this is the end!" I knelt
down near the bed. He looked at me, and
I knew somehow that we understood each
other well, that he wanted no word or
demonstration, but was just glad I was
with him. The prayers began again.
Hugh crossed himself faintly once or twice,
made a response or two. Then he said:
"I beg your pardon — one moment — my
love to them all." The big room was
brightly lit; something on the hearth boiled
over, and the nurse went across the room.
Hugh said to me: "You will make certain
I am dead, won't you?" I said "Yes,"
and then the prayers went on. Suddenly
he said to the nurse: "Nurse, is it any
good my resisting death — making any
effort?" The nurse said: "No, Monsignor; just be as quiet as you can." He
closed his eyes at this, and his breath came
quicker. Presently he opened his eyes

again and looked at me, and said in a low voice: "Arthur, don't look at me! Nurse, stand between my brother and me!" He moved his hand to indicate where she should stand. I knew well what was in his mind; we had talked not long before of the shock of certain sights, and how a dreadful experience could pierce through the reason and wound the inner spirit; and I knew that he wished to spare me the pain of seeing him die. Once or twice he drew up his hands as though trying to draw breath, and sighed a little; but there was no struggle or apparent pain. He spoke once more and said: "I commit my soul to God, to Mary, and to Joseph." The nurse had her hand upon his pulse, and presently laid his hand down, saying: "It is all over." He looked very pale and boyish then, with wide open eyes and parted lips. I kissed his hand, which was warm and firm, and went out with Canon Sharrock, who said to me: "It was wonderful! I have seen many people die, but no one ever so easily and quickly."

It was wonderful indeed! It seemed to me then, in that moment, strange rather than sad. He had been *himself* to the very end, no diminution of vigour, no yielding, no humiliation, with all his old courtesy and thoughtfulness and collectedness, and at the same time, I felt, with a real adventurousness — that is the only word I can use. I recognised that we were only the spectators, and that he was in command of the scene. He had made haste to die, and he had gone, as he was always used to do, straight from one finished task to another that waited for him. It was not like an end; it was as though he had turned a corner, and was passing on, out of sight but still unquestionably there. It seemed to me like the death of a soldier or a knight, in its calmness of courage, its splendid facing of the last extremity, its magnificent determination to experience, open-eyed and vigilant, the dark crossing.

THE CALVARY AT HARE STREET, 1913
The grave is to the left of the mound.

XVII

BURIAL

WE had thought that he should be buried at Manchester; but a paper of directions was found saying that he wished to be buried at Hare Street, in his own orchard, at the foot of his Calvary. My mother arrived on the Monday evening, and in the course of Tuesday we saw his body for the last time, in biretta and cassock, with a rosary in his hands. He looked strangely young, like a statue carved in alabaster, with no trace of pain or weariness about him, simply asleep.

His coffin was taken to the midnight train by the clergy of the Salford Cathedral and from Buntingford station by my brother Fred to his own little chapel, where it rested all the Thursday. On the Friday the Cardinal came down, with Canons from Westminster and the choir. A solemn

Requiem was sung. The Cardinal con-
secrated a grave, and he was laid there, in
the sight of a large concourse of mourners.
It was very wonderful to see them. There
were many friends and neighbours, but
there were also many others, unknown to
me and even to each other, whom Hugh
had helped and comforted in different ways,
and whose deep and visible grief testified
to the sorrow of their loss and to the
loyalty of their affection.

I spent some strange solitary days at
Hare Street in the week which followed,
going over from Cambridge and returning,
working through papers and letters. There
were all Hugh's manuscripts and notes,
his books of sermons, all the written evi-
dences of his ceaseless energy. It was an
astonishing record of diligence and patient
effort. It seemed impossible to believe
that in a life of perpetual travelling and
endless engagements he yet had been able
to accomplish all this mass of work. His
correspondence too — though he had evidently destroyed all private spiritual con-

fidences — was of wide and varied range,
and it was difficult to grasp that it yet
represented the work of so comparatively
few years. The accumulation also of little,
unknown, unnamed gifts was very great,
while the letters of grief and sympathy
which I received from friends of his, whose
very names were unknown to me, showed
how intricate and wide his personal relations had been. And yet he had carried all
this burden very lightly and easily. I
realised how wonderful his power must
have been of storing away in his mind the
secrets of many hearts, always ready to
serve them, and yet able to concentrate
himself upon any work of his own.

In his directions he spoke of his great
desire to keep his house and chapel as
much as possible in their present state.
"I have spent an immense amount of time
and care on these things," he said. It
seemed that he had nearly realised his
wish, by careful economy, to live at Hare
Street quietly and without anxiety, even
if his powers had failed him; and it was

strange to walk as I did, one day when
I had nearly finished my task, round about
the whole garden, which had been so
tangled and weed-choked a wilderness,
and the house at first so ruinous and bare,
and to realise that it was all complete and
perfect, a setting of order and peace.
How insecure and frail the beautiful hopes
of permanence and quiet enjoyment all
seemed! I passed over the smooth lawn,
under the leafless limes, through the yew-
tree walk to the orchard, where the grave
lay, with the fading wreaths, and little
paths trodden in the grass; by the hazel
hedge and the rose-garden, and the ranked
vegetable rows with their dying flower-
borders; into the chapel with its fantasy
of ornament, where the lamp burned before
the shrine; through the house, with its
silent panelled rooms all so finely ordered,
all prepared for daily use and tranquil
delight. It seemed impossible that he
should not be returning soon in joyful
haste, as he used to return, pleased to
show his new designs and additions. But

AFTER-THOUGHTS

I could not think of him as having any
shadow of regret about it all, or as coming
back, a pathetic *revenant*, to the scene of
his eager inventiveness. That was never
his way, to brood over what had been
done. It was always the new, the un-
touched, the untried, that he was in search
of. Hugh never wished that he had done
otherwise, nor did he indulge in the passion of the past, or in the half-sad, half-
luxurious retrospect of the days that are
no more. "Ah," I could fancy him saying, "that was all delightful while it lasted
— it was the greatest fun in the world!
But now!" — and I knew as well in my
heart and mind as if he had come behind
me and spoken to me, that he was moving
rapturously in some new experience of
life and beauty. He loved indeed to speak
of old days, to recall them vividly and
ecstatically, as though they were actually
present to him; and I could think of him
as even delighting to go over with me
those last hours of his life that we spent
together, not with any shadow of dread

or shrinking, but just as it pleased Odysseus to tell the tale of how he sped down the whirlpool, with death beneath and death above, facing it all, taking it all in, not cherishing any delusion of hope, and yet enjoying it as an adventure of real experience which it was good to have tasted even so.

And when I came to look at some of his letters, and saw the sweet and generous things which he had said of myself in the old days, his gratitude for trifling kindnesses and gifts which I had myself forgotten, I felt a touch of sorrow for a moment that I had not been even nearer to him than I was, and more in his enlivening company; and I remembered how, when he arrived to see me, he would come lightly in, say a word of greeting, and plunge into talk of all that we were doing; and then I felt that I must not think of him unworthily, as having any grievance or shadow of concern about my many negligences and coldnesses: but that we were bound by ties of lasting love and trust, and shared a treasure of dear memories and kindnesses; and that I might leave his spirit in its newly found activities, take up my own task in the light of his vivid example, and look forward to a day when we might be again together, sharing recollection and purpose alike, as cheerfully and gladly as we had done in the good days that were gone, with all the added joy of the new dawn, and with the old understanding made more perfect.

XVIII

PERSONAL CHARACTERISTICS

HUGH was always youthful-looking
for his age, light and quick in
movement, intent but never deliberate,
passing very rapidly from one thing to
another, impatient of boredom and dull-
ness, always desiring to do a thing that
very minute. He was fair of complexion,
with grey-blue eyes and a shock head of
light hair, little brushed, and uncut often
too long. He was careless of appearances,
and wore clothes by preference of great
shabbiness. He told me in 1909 that he
had only bought one suit in the last five
years. I have seen him, when gardening
at Hare Street, wear a pair of shoes such
as might have been picked up in a ditch
after a tramp's encampment. At the
same time he took a pleasure of a boyish
kind in robes of state. He liked his Mon-

signor's purple, his red-edged cassock and crimson cincture, as a soldier likes his uniform. He was in no way ascetic; and though he could be and often seemed to be wholly indifferent to food, yet he was amused by culinary experiments, and collected simple savoury recipes for household use. He was by far the quickest eater I have ever seen. He was a great smoker of cheap cigarettes. They were a natural sedative for his highly strung temperament. I do not think he realised how much he smoked, and he undoubtedly smoked too much for several years.

He was always quick, prompt, and decisive. He had an extraordinary presence of mind in the face of danger. My sister remembers how he was once strolling with her, in his cassock, in a lane near Tremans, when a motor came down the road at a great pace, and Roddy, the collie, trotted out in front of it, with his back turned to the car, unconscious of danger. Hugh took a leap, ran up hill, snatched Roddy up just in front of the wheels, and fell with

him against the hedge on the opposite
side of the road.

He liked a degree of comfort, and took
great pleasure in having beautiful things
about him. "I do not believe that lovely
things should be stamped upon," he once
wrote to a friend who was urging the dangers of a strong sense of beauty; adding,
"should they not rather be led in chains?"
Yet his taste was not at all severe, and
he valued things for their associations
and interest as much as he did for their
beauty. He had a great accumulation
of curious, pretty, and interesting things
at Hare Street, and took a real pleasure
in possession. At the same time he was
not in the least dependent on such things,
and could be perfectly happy in bare and
ugly rooms. There was no touch of
luxuriousness about him, and the adornment of his house was one of the games
that he played. One of his latest amusements was to equip and catalogue his
library. He was never very much of a
reader, except for a specific purpose. He

read the books that came in his way, but
he had no technical knowledge of English
literature. There were many English classics which he never looked into, and he
made no attempt to follow modern devel-
opments. But he read books so quickly
that he was acquainted more or less with
a wide range of authors. At the same time
he never wasted any time in reading books
which did not interest him, and he knew
by a sort of intuition the kind of books
he cared about.

He was of late years one of the liveliest
and most refreshing of talkers. As a boy
and a young man he was rather silent
than otherwise in the family circle, but
latterly it was just the opposite. He
talked about anything that was in his
mind, but at the same time he did not
wish to keep the talk in his own hands,
and had an eager and delighted recogni-
tion of his companion's thoughts and
ideas.

His sense of humour was unfailing, and
when he laughed, he laughed with the

whole of himself, loudly and contagiously, abandoning himself with tears in his eyes to helpless paroxysms of mirth. There was never the smallest touch of affectation or priggishness about his attitude, and he had none of the cautious and uneasy reverence which is apt to overshadow men of piety. He was intensely amused by the humorous side of the people and the institutions which he loved. Here are two slight illustrations which come back to my mind. He told me these two stories in one day at Tremans. One was that of a well-known Anglican Bishop who attended a gathering of clergy, and in his valedictory speech said that they would expect him to make some allusion to the fact that one who had attended their last meeting was no longer of the Anglican communion, having joined the Church of Rome. They would all, he said, regret the step which he had thought fit to take; but they must not forget the serious fall their poor friend had had from his bicycle not long before, which had undoubtedly

affected gravely his mental powers. Then
he told me of an unsatisfactory novice
in a religious house who had been expelled
from the community for serious faults.
His own account of it was that the reason
why he was expelled was that he used to
fall asleep at meditation, and snore so
loud that he awoke the elder brethren.

Though Hugh held things sacred, he
did not hold them inconveniently sacred,
and it did not affect their sacredness if
they had also a humorous side to them.
He had no temptation to be easily shocked,
and though he hated all impure suggestive-
ness, he could be amused by what may be
called broad humour. I always felt him
to be totally free from prudishness, and
it seemed to me that he drew the line in
exactly the right place between things that
might be funny and unrefined, and things
which were merely coarse and gross. The
fact was that he had a perfectly simple
manliness about him, and an infallible
tact, which was wholly unaffected, as to
the limits of decorum. The result was

that one could talk to him with the utmost plainness and directness. His was not a cloistered and secluded temperament. He knew the world, and had no fear of it or shrinking from it.

He dearly loved an argument, and could be both provoking and incisive. He was vehement, and hated dogmatic statements with which he did not agree. When he argued, he used a good deal of gesture, waving his hands as though to clear the air, emphasising what he said with little sweeps and openings of his hands, sometimes covering his face and leaning forwards, as if to gain time for the onset. His arguments were not so much clear as ingenious, and I never knew anyone who could defend a poor case so vigorously. When he was strained and tired, he would argue more tenaciously, and employ fantastic illustrations with great skill; but it always blew over very quickly, and as a rule he was good-tempered and reasonable enough. But he liked best a rapid and various interchange of talk. He was bored by slow-moving and solemn minds, but could extract a secret joy from pompous utterances, while nothing delighted him more than a full description of the exact talk and behaviour of affected and absurd people.

His little stammer was a very characteristic part of his manner. It was much more marked when he was a boy and a young man, and it varied much with his bodily health. I believe that it never affected him when preaching or speaking in public, though he was occasionally nervous about its doing so. It was not, so to speak, a long and leisurely stammer, as was the case with my uncle, Henry Sidgwick, the little toss of whose head as he disengaged a troublesome word, after long dallying with a difficult consonant, added a touch of *friandise* to his talk. Hugh's stammer was rather like a vain attempt to leap over an obstacle, and showed itself as a simple hesitation rather than as a repetition. He used, after a slight pause, to bring out a word with a deliberate emphasis, but it never appeared to suspend the thread of his talk. I remember an occasion, as a young man, when he took sherry, contrary to his wont, through some dinner-party; and when asked why he had done this, he said that it happened to be the only liquid the name of which he was able to pronounce on that evening. He used to feel humiliated by it, and I have heard him say, "I'm sorry — I'm stammering badly to-night!" but it would never have been very noticeable, if he had not attended to it. It is clear, however, from some of his letters that he felt it to be a real disability in talk, and even fancied that it made him absurd, though as a matter of fact the little outward dart of his head, as he forced the recalcitrant word out, was a gesture which his friends both knew and loved.

He learned to adapt himself to persons of very various natures, and indeed was so eager to meet people on their own ground that it seems to me he was to a certain extent misapprehended. I have seen a good many things said about him since his death which seem to me to be entire misinterpretations of him, arising from the simple fact that they were reflections of his companion's mood mirrored in his own sympathetic mind. Further, I am sure that what was something very like patient and courteous boredom in him, when he was confronted with some sentimental and egotistical character, was interpretated as a sad and remote unworldliness. Someone writing of him spoke of his abstracted and far-off mood, with his eyes indwelling in a rapture of hallowed thought. This seems to me wholly unlike Hugh. He was far more likely to have been considering how he could get away to something which interested him more.

Hugh's was really a very fresh and sparkling nature, never insipid, intent from morning to night on a vital enjoyment of life in all its aspects. I do not mean that he was always wanting to be amused — it was very far from that.

Amusement was the spring of his social mood; but he had a passion too for silence and solitude. His devotions were eagerly and rapturously practised; then he turned to his work. "Writing seems to me now the only thing worth doing in the world," he says in one of his letters when he was deep in a book. Then he flung himself into gardening and handicraft, back again to his writings, or his correspondence, and again to his prayers.

But it is impossible to select one of his moods, and to say that his true life lay there. His life lay in all of them. If work was tedious to him, he comforted himself with the thought that it would soon be done. He was an excellent man of affairs, never "slothful in business," but with great practical ability. He made careful bargains for his books, and looked after his financial interests tenaciously and diligently, with a definite purpose always in his mind. He lived, I am sure, always looking forward and anticipating. I do not believe he dwelt at all upon the past. It was life in which he was interested. As I walked with my mother about the beautiful garden, after his funeral, I said to her: "It seems almost too pathetic to be borne that Hugh should just have completed all this." "Yes," she said, "but I am sure we ought to think only that it meant to him seven years of very great happiness." That was perfectly true! If he had been called upon to leave Hare Street to take up some important work elsewhere, he would certainly not have dwelt on the pathetic side of it himself. He would have had a pang, as when he kissed the doorposts of his room at Mirfield on departing. But he would have gone forward, and he would have thought of it no more. He had a supreme power of casting things behind him, and he was far too intent on the present to have indulged in sentimental reveries of what had been.

It is clear to me, from what the doctors said after his death, that if the pneumonia which supervened upon great exhaustion

had been averted, he would have had to
give up much of his work for a long time,
and devote himself to rest and deliberate
idleness. I cannot conceive how he would
have borne it. He came once to be my
companion for a few days, when I was
suffering from a long period of depression
and overwork. I could do nothing except
answer a few letters. I could neither write
nor read, and spent much of my time in
the open air, and more in drowsing in
misery over an unread book. Hugh, after
observing me for a little, advised me to
work quite deliberately, and to divide up
my time among various occupations. It
would have been useless to attempt it, for
Nature was at work recuperating in her
own way by an enforced listlessness and
dreariness. But I have often since then
thought how impossible it would have been
for him to have endured such a condition.
He had nothing passive about him; and I
feel that he had every right to live his life
on his own lines, to neglect warnings, to
refuse advice. A man must find out his

own method, and take the risks which it may involve. And though I would have done and given anything to have kept him with us, and though his loss is one which I feel daily and constantly, yet I would not have it otherwise. He put into his life an energy of activity and enjoyment such as I have rarely seen. He gave his best lavishly and ungrudgingly. Even the dreadful and tragical things which he had to face he took with a relish of adventure. He has told me of situations in which he found himself, from which he only saved himself by entire coolness and decisiveness, the retrospect of which he actually enjoyed. "It was truly awful!" he would say, with a shiver of pleasing horror. But it was all worked into a rich and glowing tapestry, which he wove with all his might, and the fineness of his life seems to me to consist in this, that he made his own choices, found out the channels in which his powers could best move, and let the stream gush forth. He did not shelter himself fastidiously, or creep away out of the glare and noise. He took up the staff and scrip of pilgrimage, and, while he kept his eyes on the Celestial City, he enjoyed every inch of the way, as well the assaults and shadows and the toils as the houses of kindly entertainment, with all their curious contents, the talk of fellow-pilgrims, the arbours of refreshment, until his feet touched the brink of the river, and even there he went fearlessly forward.

XIX

RETROSPECT

NOW that I have traced the progress of Hugh's outer life from step to step, I will try to indicate what in the region of mind and soul his progress was, and I would wish to do this with particular care, even at the risk of repeating myself somewhat, because I believe that his nature was one that changed in certain ways very much; it widened and deepened greatly, and most of all in the seven last years of his life, when I believe that he found himself in the best and truest sense.

As a boy, up to the age of eighteen or nineteen, it was, I believe, a vivid and unreflective nature, much absorbed in the little pattern of life as he saw it, neither expansive nor fed upon secret visions. It was always a decided nature. He never, as a child, needed to be amused; he never

said, "What shall I do? Tell me what to
do!" He liked constant companionship,
but he had always got little businesses of
his own going on; he joined in games, and
joined keenly in them, but if a public game
was not to his taste, he made no secret
that he was bored, and, if he was released,
he went off on his own errands. I do not
remember that he ever joined in a general
game because of any sociable impulse
merely, but because it amused him; and if
he separated himself and went off, he had
no resentment nor any pathetic feeling
about being excluded.

When he went on to school he lived a
sociable but isolated life. His companions
were companions rather than friends. He
did not, I think, ever form a romantic and
adoring friendship, such as are common
enough with emotional boys. He did not
give his heart away; he just took a vivid
and animated interest in the gossip, the
interplay, the factions and parties of his
circle; but it was all rather a superficial
life — he used to say that he had neither

aims nor ambitions — he took very little
interest in his work and not much interest
in games. He just desired to escape censure, and he was not greedy of praise.
There was nothing listless or dreamy about
it all. If he neglected his work, it was
because he found talk and laughter more
interesting. No string ran through his
days; they were just to be taken as they
came, enjoyed, dismissed. But he never
wanted to appear other than he was, or to
be admired or deferred to. There was
never any sense of pose about him nor the
smallest affectation. He was very indifferent as to what was thought of him, and
not sensitive; but he held his own, and
insisted on his rights, allowed no dictation,
followed no lead. All the time, I suppose,
he was gathering in impressions of the out-
sides of things — he did not dip beyond
that: he was full of quite definite tastes,
desires, and prejudices; and though he was
interested in life, he was not particularly
interested in what lay behind it. He was
not in the least impressionable, in the sense

that others influenced or diverted him
from his own ideas.

Neither had he any strong intellectual
bent. The knowledge which he needed he
acquired quickly and soon forgot it. I do
not think he ever went deeply into things
in those early days, or tried to perfect himself in any sort of knowledge. He was
neither generous nor acquisitive; he was
detached, and always rather apt to put his
little possessions away and to forget about
them. It was always the present he was
concerned with; he did not deal with the
past nor with the future.

Then after what had been not so much a
slumber of the spirit as a vivid living
among immediate impressions, the artistic
nature began to awake in him. Music,
architecture, ceremony, began to make
their appeal felt; and he then first recognised the beauty of literary style. But
even so, he did not fling himself creatively
into any of these things at first, even as an
amateur; it was still the perception of
effects that he was concerned with.

VOCATION

It was then, during his first year at Cambridge, that the first promptings of a vocation made themselves felt towards the priesthood. But he was as yet wholly unaware of his powers of expression; and I am sure that his first leanings to the clerical life were a search for a quiet and secluded fortress, away from the world, in which he might pursue an undisturbed and ordered life of solemnity and delicate impressions of a sacred sort of beauty. His desire for community life was caused by his decided dislike of the world, of fuss and tedium and conventional occupations. He was never in the least degree a typical person. He had no wish to be distinguished, or to influence other minds or lives, or to gain honour or consideration. These things simply appeared to him as not worth striving for. What he desired was companionship of a sympathetic kind and the opportunity of living among the pursuits he liked best. He never wished to try experiments, and it was always with a spectacular interest that he regarded the world.

His call was very real, and deeply felt, and he waited for a whole year to make sure of it; but he found full decision at last.

Then came his first ministerial work at the Eton Mission; and this did not satisfy him; his strength emerged in the fact that he did not adopt or defer to the ideals he found about him: a weaker character would have embraced them half-heartedly, tried to smother its own convictions, and might have ended by habituating itself to a system. But Hugh was still, half unconsciously, perhaps, in search of his real life; he did not profess to be guided by anyone, nor did he ever suspend his own judgment as to the worth of what he was doing; a manly and robust philanthropy on Christian lines was not to his taste. His instinct was rather for the beautiful element in religion and in life, and for a mystical consecration of all to God. That did not seem to him to be recognised in the work which he was doing. If he had been less independent, he might have crushed it

down, and come to view it as a private
fancy. He might have said to himself
that it was plain that many human spirits
did not feel that more delicate appeal, and
that his duty was to meet other natures
on some common ground.

It is by such sacrifices of personal bias
that much of the original force of the
world is spoiled and wasted. It may be a
noble sacrifice, and it is often nobly made.
But Hugh was not cast in that mould.
His effectiveness was to lie in the fact
that he could disregard many ordinary
motives. He could frankly admire other
methods of work, and yet be quite sure
that his own powers did not lie in that
direction. But though he was modest and
not at all self-assertive, he never had the
least submissiveness nor subservience; nor
was he capable of making any pretences.

Sometimes it seems to happen that men
are punished for wilfulness of choice by
missing great opportunities. A nature
which cannot compromise anything, cannot
ignore details, cannot work with others, is

sometimes condemned to a fruitless isolation. But it would be wrong to disregard the fact that circumstances more than once came to Hugh's aid; I see very clearly how he was, so to speak, headed off, as by some Fatherly purpose, from wasting his life in ineffectual ways. Probably he might have worked on at the Eton Mission, might have lost heart and vigour, might never have discovered his real powers, if he had not been rescued. His illness at this juncture cut the knot for him; and then followed a time of travel in Egypt, in the Holy Land, which revived again his sense of beauty and width and proportion.

And then followed his Kemsing curacy; I have a letter written to me from Kemsing in his first weeks there, in which he describes it as a paradise and says that, so far as he can see, it is exactly the life he most desires, and that he hopes to spend the rest of his days there.

But now I feel that he took a very real step forward. The danger was that he would adopt a dilettante life. He had still

[238]

not discovered his powers of expression,
which developed late. He was only just
beginning to preach with effect, and his
literary power was practically undeveloped.
He might have chosen to live a harmless,
quiet, beauty-loving life, kindly and guileless, in a sort of religious æstheticism;
though the vivid desire for movement and
even excitement that characterised his
later life would perhaps have in any case
developed.

But something stronger and sterner
awoke in him. I believe that it was
exactly because the cup, mixed to his
taste, was handed to him that he was
able to see that there was nothing that
was invigorating about the potion. It was
not the community life primarily which
drew him to Mirfield; it was partly that
his power of speech awoke, and more
strongly still the idea of self-discipline.

And so he went to Mirfield, and then all
his powers came with a rush in that
studious, sympathetic, and ascetic atmosphere. He was in his twenty-eighth year.

He began by finding that he could preach
with real force and power, and two years
later, when he wrote *The Light Invisible*,
he also discovered his gift of writing;
while as a little recreation, he took up
drawing, and produced a series of sketches,
full of humour and delicacy, drawn with
a fine pen and tinted with coloured chalk,
which are at all events enough to show
what he could have done in this direction.

XX

ATTAINMENT

AND then Hugh made the great change of his life, and, as a Catholic, found his dreams realized and his hopes fulfilled. He found, indeed, the life which moves and breathes inside of every faithful creed, the power which supplements weakness and represses distraction, the motive for glad sacrifice and happy obedience. I can say this thankfully enough, though in many ways I confess to being at the opposite pole of religious thought. He found relief from decision and rest from conflict. He found sympathy and confidence, a sense of corporate union, and above all a mystical and symbolical devotion embodied in a great and ancient tradition, which was visibly and audibly there with a movement like a great tide, instead of a scheme of worship which had, he thought,

in the Anglican Church, to be eclectically
constructed by a group or a circle. Every
part of his nature was fed and satisfied;
and then, too, he found in the Roman
Catholic community in England that sort
of eager freemasonry which comes of the
desire to champion a cause that has won a
place for itself, and influence and respect,
but which is yet so much opposed to
national tendencies as to quicken the sense
of active endeavour and eager expectation.

After his quiet period of study and
thought in Rome and at Llandaff House,
came the time when he was attached to
the Roman Catholic Church in Cambridge;
and this, though not congenial to him,
gave him an insight into methods and conditions; and all the while his own forces
and qualities were learning how to concentrate and express themselves. He learned
to write, he learned to teach, to preach, to
speak, to be his own natural self, with all
his delicate and ingenuous charm, in the
presence of a great audience; so that when
at last his opportunity came to free himself

from official and formal work, he was able
to throw all his trained faculties into the
work which he had at heart. Moreover,
he found in direction and confession, and
in careful discussion with inquirers, and in
sympathetic aid given to those in trouble,
many of the secret sorrows, hopes, and
emotions of the human heart, so that his
public work was enforced and sustained by
his ever-increasing range of private experience.

He never, however, took whole-heartedly
to pastoral work. He said frankly that he
"specialised" in the region of private direction and advice; but I doubt if he ever did
quite enough general pastoral work of a
commonplace and humdrum kind to supplement and fill out his experience of
human nature. He never knew people
under quite normal conditions, because he
felt no interest in normal conditions. He
knew men and women best under the more
abnormal emotion of the confessional; and
though he used to maintain, if challenged,
that penitence was a normal condition, yet

his judgment of human beings was, as a consequence, several times gravely at fault. He made some unwise friendships, with a guileless curiosity, and was obliged, more than once, to extricate himself by summary abandonments.

He wrote of himself once, "I am tired to death of giving myself away, and finding out too late. . . I don't like my tendency to agree with people wildly; my continual fault has been to put on too much fuel." Like all sensitive people, who desire sympathetic and friendly relations, he was apt to discover the best of new acquaintances at once, and to evoke in them a similarly genial response. It was not till later, when the first conciliatory impulse had died down, that he discovered the faults that had been instinctively concealed, and indeed repressed by his own personal attractiveness.

He had, too, an excessive confidence in his power of managing a critical situation, and several times undertook to reform people in whom corruption had gone too far for remedy. He believed in his power of "breaking" sinners by stern declarations; but he had more than once to confess himself beaten, though he never wasted time in deploring failures.

Mr. Meynell, in his subtle essay which prefaces my brother's little book of poems, speaks of the complete subjugation of his will. If I may venture to express a different view, I do not feel that Hugh ever learned to efface his own will. I do not think his temperament was made on the lines of self-conquest. I should rather say that he had found the exact *milieu* in which he could use his will to the best effect, so that it was like the charge of powder within the gun, no longer exploding itself vaguely and aimlessly, but all concentrated upon one intense and emissive effort. Because the one characteristic of the last years of his life was his immense enjoyment of it all. He wrote to a friend not long before the end, when he was feeling the strain upon him to be heavier than he could bear; after a word or two about the war — he had

volunteered to go to the front as a chaplain — he said, "So I am staying here as
usual; but the incessant demands on my
time try me as much as shrapnel and
bullets." That sentence seems to me to
confirm my view that he had not so much
sacrificed as devoted himself. He never
gained a serene patience; I have heard him
over and over again speak with a sigh of
his correspondence and the demands it
made on him; yet he was always faithful
to a relation once formed; and the number
of letters written to single correspondents,
which have been sent me, have fairly
amazed me by their range, their freshness, and their fulness. He was deeply
interested in many of the letters he received, and gave his best in his prompt
replies; but he evidently also received an
immense number of letters from people
who did not desire guidance so much as
sympathy and communication. The inconsiderate egotism of unimaginative and
yet sensitive people is what creates the
burden of such a correspondence; and

though he answered his letters faithfully
and duly, and contrived to say much in
short space, yet he felt, as I have heard
him say, that people were merciless;
and much of the time he might have devoted to creative work, or even to recreation, was consumed in fruitless toil of
hand and mind. And yet I am sure that
he valued the sense that he could be use-
ful and serviceable, and that there were
many who depended upon him for advice
and consolation. I believe that his wide-
spread relations with so many desirous
people gave him a real sense of the fulness
and richness of life and its relations. But
for all that, I also believe that his courtesy
and his sense of duty were even more
potent in these relations than the need of
personal affection. I do not mean that
there was any hardness or coldness about
him; but he valued sympathy and tranquil
friendship more than he pursued intimacy
and passionate devotion. Yet in the last
year or two of his life, I was both struck
and touched by his evident desire to knit

up friendships which had been severed, and
to renew intercourse which had been suspended by his change of belief. Whether
he had any feeling that his life was pre-
carious, or his own time short, I do not
know. He never said as much to me. He
had, of course, used hard words of the
Church which he had left, and had said
things which were not wholly impersonal.
But, combative though he was, he had no
touch of rancour or malice in his nature,
and he visibly rejoiced in any sign of
goodwill.

Yet even so, he was essentially solitary
in mind. "When I am alone," he once
wrote, "I am at my best; and at my worst
in company. I am happy and capable in
loneliness; unhappy, distracted, and inef-
fective in company." And again he wrote,
"I am becoming more and more afraid of
meeting people I want to meet, because my
numerous deficiencies are so very apparent.
For example, I stammer slightly always
and badly at times."

This was, I believe, more an instinctive

shrinking from the expenditure of nervous force than anything else, and arose from the feeling that, if he had to meet strangers, some brilliancy of contribution would be expected of him. I remember how he delighted in the story of Marie Bashkirtseff, who, when she was summoned to meet a party of strangers who desired to see her, prayed as she entered the room, "Oh God, make me worth seeing!" Hugh disliked the possibility of disappointing expectations, and thus found the society of unfamiliar people a strain; but in family life, and with people whom he knew well, he was always the most delightful and charming of companions, quick, ready, and untiring in talk. And therefore I imagine that, like all artistic people, he found that the pursuit of some chosen train of thought was less of a conscious effort to him than the necessity of adapting himself, swiftly and dexterously, to new people, whose mental and spiritual atmosphere he was obliged to observe and infer. It was all really a sign of the high pressure at which he lived, and of the price he paid for his vividness and animation.

Another source of happiness to him in these last days was his sense of power. This was a part of his artistic nature; and I believe that he enjoyed to the full the feeling of being able to give people what they wanted, to enchant, interest, move, and sway them. This is to some natures a great temptation, because they come to desire applause, and to hunger for tangible signs of their influence. But Hugh was marvellously saved from this, partly by a real modesty which was not only never marred, but which I used to think increased with the years. There is a story of William Morris, that he could read aloud his own poetry, and at the end of a fine stanza would say: "That's jolly!" with an entire freedom from conceit, just as dispassionately as he could praise the work of another. I used to feel that when Hugh mentioned, as I have heard him do, some course of sermons that he was giving, and described the queue which formed in the street, and the aisles

ROBERT HUGH BENSON

IN 1912.   AGED 40

ENERGY

and gangways crowded with people standing to hear him, that he did so more imper-
sonally than anyone I had ever heard, as
though it were a delightful adventure, and
more a piece of good luck than a testimony
to his own powers.

It was the same with his books; he
wished them to succeed and enjoyed their
success, while it was an infinite delight to
him to write them. But he had no egotism
of a commonplace sort about him, and he
never consciously tried to succeed. Success
was just the reverberating echo of his own
delight.

And thus I do not look upon him as one
who had bent and curbed his nature by
stern self-discipline to do work of a heavy
and distasteful kind; nor do I think that
his dangerous devotion to work was the
fierce effort of a man who would have
wished to rest, yet felt that the time was
too short for all that he desired to do. I
think it was rather the far more fruitful
energy of one who exulted in expressing
himself, in giving a brilliant and attract-

[251]

ive shape to his ideas, and who loved, too, the varieties and tendencies of human nature, enjoyed moulding and directing them, and flung himself with an intense joy of creation into all the work which he found ready to his hand.

XXI

TEMPERAMENT

HUGH never seemed to me to treat life in the spirit of a mystic or a dreamer, with unshared and secret experiences, withdrawing into his own ecstasy, half afraid of life, rapt away into interior visions. Though he had a deep curiosity about mystical experiences, he was never a mystic in the sense that he had, as great mystics seem to have had, one shell less, so to speak, between him and the unseen. He lived in the visible and tangible world, loving beautiful secrets; and he was a mystic only in the sense that he had an hourly and daily sense of the presence of God. He wished to share his dreams and to make known his visions, to declare the glory of God and to show His handiwork. He found the world more and more interesting, as he came to know it, and in the light of the warm welcome it gave him. He had a keen and delicate apprehension of spiritual beauty, and the Mass became to him a consummation of all that he held most holy and dear. He had recognised a mystical presence in the Church of England, but he found a supernatural presence in the Church of Rome; yet he had, too, the instinct of the poet, to translate into form and substance his inmost and sweetest joy, and to lavish it upon others. No one dares to speak of great poets and seers as men who have profaned a mystery by making it known. The deeper that the poet's sense of beauty is, the more does he thirst to communicate it. It is far too divine and tremendous to be secretly and selfishly enjoyed.

It is possible, of course, that Hugh may have given to those who did not see him constantly in everyday familiar intercourse, the sense of a courteous patience and a desire to do full justice to a claim. Still

more may he have given this impression
on social occasions and at conventional
gatherings. Interviews and so-called fes-
tivities were apt to be a weariness to him,
because they seemed so great an expenditure of time and force for very scanty
results; but I always felt him to be one of
the most naturally courteous people I have
ever seen. He hated to be abrupt, to repel,
to hurt, to wound feelings, to disappoint;
yet on such occasions his natural courtesy
was struggling with a sense of the waste of
time involved and the interruptions caused.
I remember his writing to me from the
Catholic rectory when he was trying to
finish a book and to prepare for a course
of sermons, and lamenting that he was
"driven almost mad" by ceaseless interviews with people who did not, he declared,
want criticism or advice, but simply the
luxury of telling a long story for the sake
of possible adulation. "I am quite ready
to see people," he added, "if only they
would ask me to appoint a time, instead
of simply flinging themselves upon me

whenever it happens to be convenient to them."

I do not think he ever grudged the time to people in difficulties when he felt he could really help and save. That seemed to him an opportunity of using all his powers; and when he took a soul in hand, he could display a certain sternness, and even ruthlessness, in dealing with it. "You need not consult me at all, but if you do you must carry out exactly what I tell you," he could say; but he did grudge time and attention given to mild sentimentalists, who were not making any way, but simply dallying with tragic emotions excitedly and vainly.

This courtesy was part of a larger quality, a certain knightly and chivalrous sense, which is best summed up in the old word "gentleman." A priest told me that soon after Hugh's death he had to rebuke a tipsy Irishman, who was an ardent Catholic and greatly devoted to Hugh. The priest said, "Are you not ashamed to think that Monsignor's eye may be on you now, and that he may see how you disgrace yourself?" To which, he said, the Irishman replied, with perhaps a keener insight into Hugh's character than his director, "Oh no, I can trust Monsignor not to take advantage of me. I am sure that he will not come prying and spying about. He always believed whatever I chose to tell him, God bless him!" Hugh could be hard and unyielding on occasions, but he was wholly incapable of being suspicious, jealous, malicious, or spiteful. He made friends once with a man of morbid, irritable, and resentful tendencies, who had continued, all his life, to make friends by his brilliance and to lose them by his sharp, fierce, and contemptuous animosities. This man eventually broke with him altogether, and did his best by a series of ingenious and wicked letters to damage Hugh's character in all directions. I received one of those documents and showed it to Hugh. I was astonished at his courage and even indifference. I myself should have been anxious and despondent at the thought of such evil innuendoes and gross misrepresentations being circulated, and still more at the sort of malignant hatred from which they proceeded. Hugh took the letter and smiled. "Oh," he said, "I have put my case before the people who matter, and you can't do anything. He is certainly mad, or on the verge of madness. Don't answer it — you will only be drenched with these communications. I don't trouble my head about it." "But don't you mind?" I said. "No," he said, "I'm quite callous! Of course I am sorry that he should be such a beast, but I can't help that. I have done my best to make it up — but it is hopeless." And it was clear from the way he changed the subject that he had banished the whole matter from his mind. At a later date, when the letters to him grew more abusive, I was told by one who was living with him, that he would even put one up on his chimney-piece and point it out to visitors.

I always thought that he had a very conspicuous and high sort of courage, not

ROBERT HUGH BENSON

IN 1912.   AGED 41

only in facing disagreeable and painful things, but in not dwelling on them either before or after. This was never more entirely exemplified than by the way he faced his operation, and indeed, most heroically of all, in the way in which he died. There was a sense of great adventure — there is no other word for it — about that, as of a man going on a fateful voyage; a courage so great that he did not even lose his interest in the last experiences of life. His demeanour was not subdued or submissive; he did not seem to be asking for strength to bear or courage to face the last change. He was more like the happy warrior

> "Attired
> With sudden brightness, as a man inspired."

He did not lose control of himself, nor was he carried helplessly down the stream. He was rather engaged in a conflict which was not a losing one. He had often thought of death, and even thought that he feared it; but now that it was upon him he would taste it fully, he would see what it was like.

The day before, when he thought that he
might live, there was a pre-occupation over
him, as though he were revolving the
things he desired to do; but when death
came upon him unmistakably there was no
touch of self-pity or impressiveness. He
had just to die, and he devoted his swift
energies to it, as he had done to living. I
never saw him so splendid and noble as he
was at that last awful moment. Life did
not ebb away, but he seemed to fling it
from him, so that it was not as the death
of a weary man sinking to rest, but like
the eager transit of a soldier to another
part of the field.

"Could it have been avoided?" I said
to the kind and gentle doctor who saw
Hugh through the last days of his life,
and loved him very tenderly and faithfully. "Well, in one sense, 'yes,'" he
replied. "If he had worked less, rested
more, taken things more easily, he might
have lived longer. He had a great vitality; but most people die of being themselves; and we must all live as we are

made to live. It was Monsignor's way
to put the work of a month into a week;
he could not do otherwise — I cannot
think of Monsignor as sitting with folded
hands."

INDEX

HUGH

INDEX

THE · PLIMPTON · PRESS
NORWOOD · MASS · U · S · A